BREAK FREE

52 Tips to Escape from Your Self Imposed Prison

by

Faith Saunders

TABLE OF CONTENTS

"You Have to **BE** *Before You Can Do, Do Before You Can Have."*
- Zig Ziglar -

PONDER THIS$_{19}$ Your Past

"You Have to Be Before You Can Do, **DO** *Before You Can Have."*
- Zig Ziglar -

"You Have to Be Before You Can Do, Do Before You Can **HAVE**.*"*
- Zig Ziglar -

Thank you!

ABOUT

52 Tips to Escape from Your Self Imposed Prison

This book has been a long time coming. I tried about 7 years ago to write it but had to put it aside because I felt that I was not writing from my soul. In other words, I was writing what I thought other people wanted to hear. In introspect, I had a whole lot of work to do – my wounds were still healing and some of them were oozing because I was not at a place emotionally that I could attend to them. Long story short, I was not ready or willing to do the 'personal' work that was needed to share at that time. *I was still in my self-imposed prison.*

This book is a testimony of the work that I have done and still continue to do because I, like you, am a work in progress and will continue to be until I take my last breath. This is one of the main messages that I would like to convey in this book. We are all a work in progress. The sooner we accept this the sooner we will truly start living and get the most out of this journey called life. We are not perfect and certainly no one has all the answers. Therefore, it's okay to explore and learn because that is how we can grow healthier and stronger.

Fortunately, many of us have never put a foot in a physical prison but unfortunately we live in one. I sometime wonder which is worst because at least the physical bars are there to prevent us from leaving; however, emotional bars are hidden and more challenging to identify and overcome. These emotional bars keep us hostage and prevents us from living the life that we are meant to live. Our bars are made up of shame, self-limiting thoughts, fear, what people are going to say, self-sabotaging behaviors... the list goes on.

I have heard that most prisoners profess innocence – they were falsely imprisoned and blame others for their situation. I can identify! My situation was due to my parents, my job, being an immigrant, being abused, depression, etc. I was not willing to take personal responsibility for my life. If you take nothing else away from this book, please take this - **YOU ARE RESPONSIBLE FOR YOUR** LIFE!

I have come to realize that, although we are individuals, we have so... much in common. We're NOT alone with our struggles. The sad thing is that we *think* that we are. Hence, we stay in silos with our hurt and pain when we could support each other and heal together!

Over the past couple of years, especially 2013, I have done a great deal of work. It involved taking a serious look at my life and facing my gremlins. It was very painful but what I realized was that I had a whole lot going for me that was masked by this other stuff. Today, I am much better. Totally healed – definitely not! However, I am definitely in a healthier space because I am embracing all facets of myself and as a result, I am showing up as my authentic self; not who I want people to think I am.

My prayer is that the exercises in this book will guide you through a self-discovery experience and empower you to be all that God has in store for you. You'll realize that *you have it going on* and that you have disowned and unrecognized qualities and strengths that are just waiting to be uncovered and utilized.

Well, are you open, ready and willing to go on this journey? If you have read this far, I think you are.

HOW TO USE

52 Tips to Escape from Your Self Imposed Prison

I struggled with the format of this book for quite a while. I finally decided to do a workbook format because there are so many inspiring books on the market but, people are still not doing the work to get unstuck or move forward. Hence, this book is for individuals who are <u>ready</u>, <u>willing</u> and <u>able</u> to do the work that is needed to be the best version of them self.

Each chapter of this book - *52 Tips to Escape from Your Self Imposed Prison!* is meant to challenge you to take an introspective look at your life and answer the question, "Am I being the best version of myself?" This is a rhetorical question and one only you can answer. For the healing to really start, you have to *'tell the truth'* - as one of my favorite persons, Iyanla Vanzant, would say!

My goal is also to help you to identify your treasures, those qualities that are inside of you that distinguish you from everyone else - and OWN them. To do this, you have to be willing to BE. What I mean is that you have to be willing to **stop doing and just be** with yourself.

Let me explain a little more - Zig Ziglar introduced the BE, DO, HAVE paradigm years ago. It says that many people believe that they need to continuously **"DO"** - *work none stop, socialize with a certain group of people and be in certain environments and so forth* so that they can **"HAVE"** things - *money, love, the perfect job, clothes, a fancy house, cars, etc.* - so that they can **"BE"** - *peaceful, loved, successful, ...* However, it works the other way around.

First we need to **"BE"** which involves connecting with the core of who we are, so that we can **"DO"** what really brings us joy and meaning. Soon we discover that what we're doing yields the things that we've always wanted to **"HAVE"** and are important to us.

This sounds easy but for many it's not. It's scary as that's when those ugly gremlins appear. I can relate to this in so many ways because this was me until a few years ago. I was constantly doing something. I got so many accolades because to the world I was 'driven, hardworking, ambitious...' This fueled my need to achieve but unbeknown to many, this was my way of hiding because being quiet was too painful.

This book will be subdivided into 3 sections. Each section will have activities geared at helping you to BE by connecting with the real essence of who you are, DO what you need to do to fulfill your purpose and HAVE the things that are important to you.

Next, I suggest that you get a notebook and use it as you go through this book. This is important for many reasons:

1. It will help you to organize your thoughts and uncover things about yourself that are lurking in your subconscious. Studies say that we have between **50,000 – 70,000 thoughts per DAY!** Can you imagine? How many of these are you aware of? Do you get my point! Writing helps us unclutter and tap into some of the good stuff that can help us break free and also identify some of the bars that are keeping us prisoners.
2. It helps you to document your journey and have a point of reference, something you can look back on and see from *whence you came*. This point may seem funny but it can be very empowering. Believe me, there are going to be times when you revert to your old habits and feel stuck.

Going back and looking at your journey can and will give you the nudge you need to move forward.

3. It is imperative that you nurture yourself during this process. Transitioning from the old to the new is not easy and involves hard work which is emotionally and physically draining. You will need to take a break. Do something nice for yourself. This should be fun and easy to do but again, for some it isn't. "Why?" you may ask. Answer, *drum roll...* they don't think they deserve to be treated nicely. Of course, we often blame the age old *enemy* – **TIME!**

I feel compelled to add that nurturing yourself does not have to involve spending money, especially if you're in debt. Be creative, you will be surprise what you will come up with.

Finally, this book is meant to be used in conjunction with **Ponder This₂ Notes** - 52 inspirational messages from the Messages in a Tin collection. They are meant to be a reminder of what you're working to accomplish as you go about your everyday life. They are also meant to encourage, inspiration as well as challenge your thinking. They are packaged in a small tin so that you can keep them on your desk, in your car or easily carry them with you anywhere!

So without further ado, let's break free by removing the bars from your cell one by one!

Acknowledgment
"Thank you is the best prayer that one can say."
Alice Walker

First and foremost, I want to thank my Higher Power – **God**. This may sound so cliché but without Him I'm NOTHING. He and I have had several conversations and disagreements during this journey as I try to do things my way or when I try to shun my responsibility as it relates to writing. One lesson I have come to learn is that even when I felt alone, confused, frustrated, scared... He was there. Those valleys helped to mold me to do His work. So again, thank you Heavenly Father.

Next, my family – especially my parents, **Belville** (deceased) and **Edna Saunders.** Thank you! These words may sound so simple but they are saturated with gratitude. A large part of who I am today is due to my upbringing – spiritual background, strong work ethic, and a need to contribute to the larger world. Not only did you lead by words but you modeled by your actions. When I was young, I must be honest and say that many of the things you said were quite annoying. However, as an adult, I frequently repeat so many of the sayings that I grew up hearing because they are so true. I repeat this one a lot - *"Mout mek fi sey any ting."* This is our Jamaica dialect that translates – "you can tell anyone what they want to hear but what really counts is your actions."

My siblings, I love you all. Thanks for your love and continuous support in so many ways. Other family members, you're too many to mention but you know who you are – thanks so much for all that you do. It means a lot and is greatly appreciated.

My friends for all of your encouragement. You know who you are - thank you cannot express how much your friendship means to me. I however have to acknowledge two friends by name. **Deborah Bailey** who has been my coach through this whole process and eventually my editor. Experience is the greatest teacher and with 4 books under your belt, your wisdom and guidance have definitely helped me to make this book a reality. **Serene Longsworth** for proofreading, working through the exercises and giving me constructive feedback.

Last, but DEFINITELY NOT LEAST – my children, **Daniel and Ashley**. You have heard me say this before but I am putting it in writing. Parents are meant to raise kids but as parents, if we are open, we can learn a whole lot from our kids. I have learned so much from you both. I love you so much. I thank God every day for choosing me to be your mother.

I love you all and God's continuous blessings be with you.

YOU HAVE TO

BE

BEFORE YOU CAN DO,

DO

BEFORE YOU

HAVE

Zig Ziglar

Identifying the Bars of Our Self Imposed Prison
"You're still in prison if you do nothing better in freedom."
Toba Beta

BAR: DISHONESTY

One of the jobs that I had earlier in my career was that of a Visitation Specialist. I would take children who were in the foster care system to visit their parents and/or siblings. During the visit, I would observe their interaction and write a report. One of my clients was a baby who was just a few months old. Both her parents were incarcerated and so I had to take this beautiful baby to visit them in jail. Both the baby and I were searched each time we went. I felt so violated and even more upsetting to me was seeing the parents brought out in handcuffs. They were not allowed to visit together. One would visit first, and when he/she was taken back to their cell, the other was brought in.

I cannot imagine -- and don't want to imagine -- what it would be like to be incarcerated and lose my freedom. Little did I realize that although I wasn't in a physical cell, the way I was living my life came pretty close. I was imprisoned by my thoughts and behaviors. Sounds weird right? But it's not.

Now that I am in a healthier space, I realize that many people who are incarcerated took risks and participated in behaviors that landed them there. The problem is that their choices were not the right ones.

Many people are walking around free - but are they? They can do anything (almost anything) they desire but they are imprisoned by their imposed cells and are totally frustrated and miserable. This isn't something to be ashamed of because we are all on a journey called life, and each of us is on our own separate path. Though this journey is personal, we can all learn from each other. Sometime one small insight can make a difference and help us to break free.

Faulty Beliefs	Your Past	Negative Attitude	Selfish-ness	Depress-ion	Self-Pity
Envy	Unfor-giveness	Anger	People Pleaser	Fear	Procras-tination
Pride	Guilt	Self-Neglect	Shame	Dishon-esty	Lack of Vision
Self-Sabotage	Regrets	Poor Planning	No Action	Unclear Purpose	Poor Time Manage-ment

Below is a drawing of a prison cell with words that describe some of the things (bars) that keep us hostage.

1. Review it and circle the cells that are keeping you from living your best life. If there are others that are not listed, please write them in the section below.

OTHERS BARS:

* _____

- _____
- _____
- _____
- _____
- _____

2. **Identify your top three (3) bars below and describe how they have held you back.**

   BAR #1:_____

   Keeps me imprisoned in the following ways

   _____
   _____
   _____
   _____
   _____
   _____
   _____
   _____
   _____
   _____
   _____
   _____
   _____
   _____

   BAR #2: _____

Keeps me imprisoned in the following ways

_____

_____

_____

_____

_____

_____

_____

_____

_____

_____

_____

BAR #3: _____

Keeps me imprisoned in the following ways

_____

_____

_____

_____

_____

_____

_____

_____

_____

_____

_____

_____

_____

I LEARNED THAT…

_____

_____

_____

_____

Tip: *The first step to breaking free is to be honest with yourself.*

PONDER THIS₂
Our Beliefs Go A Long... Way!
"Whatever follows "I am" represents what you're putting out in the universe."
Faith Saunders

BAR: FAULTY BELIEFS

WHO AM I?
(Written by Faith Saunders)

A PERSON
A soul who is traveling this journey call life
Sharing, exploring, and questioning the many facets of my existence.
A person with many roles
Mother, daughter, sister, aunt, cousin, friend, employee...
The list goes on and on
A person with emotions, at times, too many to decipher
Happiness, sadness, utopia, anger...
Sometimes, they seem to all roll into one
A person blessed with many creative outlets
Writer, poet, speaker, actress, dancer...
Some I have yet to uncover
So... try to see me for who I am!
A complex, unique and special
I-N-D-I-V-I-D-U-A-L!
Searching for the meaning of life while playing many roles,
Experiencing many emotions and utilizing many creative outlets!

One day, while I was in my valley, I realized that one key to getting out is to answer the question – **"Who Am I?"** This question got me frustrated because I couldn't define it with one word. In addition, my perceptual lens were very tainted. I was too busy beating up on myself - what I didn't have, what I couldn't do, what I was told by others and so forth - that I could not see/think clearly. This caused a considerable amount of inner turmoil. This particular valley experience helped me to answer the question and put me on the path to self-discovery.

I began to see that there is no one word to define who I am (and who you are) because we are complex human beings so we cannot be neatly put into a box; hence, the above poem. I also came to realize that who I am will continuously change as I live my life. I am growing and learning new things about the world and myself each day. This journey will not end until I breathe my last breath.

In addition, who you and I are is not based primarily upon titles, accolades and so forth. These things are but a minute piece of who we are. This way of thinking encourages us to get into trouble because when they are gone, we are left feeling naked, empty and alone. Since we live in a culture that highly values what people do for a living and how much money one has, it's easy to get caught up in that trap. Case in point, when the economy tanked years ago - many baby boomers who had prestigious positions and longevity at their jobs lost them. Some still have not recuperated from this loss because the premise upon which they defined themselves is gone.

The opening poem was one that I wrote earlier on in this quest of self – discovery. It is a reminder to me that there is so much of who I am that is yet to be uncovered and untapped. In fact, the original title was – *Don't Put Me in a Box*. Well, it's your turn! How do you see yourself?

Find a quiet space and in your journal/notebook complete the following sentence. Don't think; just write for 15 minutes

anything that comes to mind. You'll be surprised what shows up on paper! (Use additional paper if needed.)

"I AM …

_____

_____

_____

_____

_____

_____

_____

_____

_____

_____

_____

_____

_____

_____

_____

_____

_____

_____

_____

_____

_____

_____

_____

_____

_____

_____

_____

_____

_____

_____

_____

_____

_____

_____

_____

I LEARNED THAT...

_____

_____

_____

Tip: Be clear about who you are and own it.

Fold the page or paper and put it aside. We will be coming back to it later.

PONDER THIS₃

There Is More to You Than You Think!

"You have to discover you, what you do, and trust it!"

Barbara Streisand

BAR: LOW SELF- ESTEEM

As Barbara Streisand said in the above quote - *"You have to discover you, what you do, and trust it!"* We have the resources to manifest what it is that we are here to do, but if you are like the old Faith - that's me – you wanted to know every detail beforehand. I have missed out on many opportunities by wasting precious time trying to figure out the details beforehand, or worrying about what would have happen if...

However, I don't have regrets because I did what I did based upon what I knew at the time.

Today, I realize that trying to figure out the minute details in advance is useless. I cannot predict the future and have no control over it. Many times things don't work out the way I planned because some unforeseen event occurs. However - somewhere, somehow - I find a way to overcome whatever the obstacle is and the outcomes are better than my original plan.

Take a few minutes and answer the following questions:
1. **If you had no limitations - money, time, responsibilities, support, etc. (these are the thing we often blame for preventing us from accomplishing our goals) what would you be doing with your life?**

_____

_____

_____

_____

_____

_____

_____

_____

_____

_____

2. **What is currently preventing you from pursuing this dream?**

_____

_____

_____

_____

_____

_____

_____

_____

_____

I LEARNED THAT…

_____

_____

_____

Tip: You are lovable and capable.

PONDER THIS$_4$

How Do You Want To Be Remembered?
"That is your legacy on this Earth when you leave this Earth: how many hearts you touched."
Patti Davis

BAR: NO VISION

If you had the opportunity to attend your funeral, what would you like to hear? Is the way you're currently living your life designed to yield the outcome you'd like? One way to ascertain if you are on track is to write your own obituary.

My Tribute

1. Write a tribute that reflects your life to date:

_____

_____

_____

_____

_____

_____

_____

_____

_____

_____

_____

_____

_____

_____

_____

_____

_____

_____

_____

_____

_____

2. Continue writing your Tribute. This time write a fantasy
   one - include all the things you wish you had done with
   your life.

_____

_____

_____

_____

_____

_____

_____

_____

_____

_____

_____

_____

_____

_____

_____

_____

3. Now it is time to really ponder what you wrote by asking yourself the following questions.

    a. If I took my last breath today, would I be happy about the life I led? *Explain*

_____

_____

_____

_____

_____

_____

_____

_____

_____

_____

    b. Am I satisfied with the direction in which my life is going?

_____

_____

_____

_____

_____

_____

_____

_____

_____

_____

c. What's missing?

_____

_____

_____

_____

_____

_____

_____

_____

_____

_____

_____

I LEARNED THAT...

_____

_____

_____

Tip: Live your life so that you have no regrets!

PONDER THIS$_5$

You're More Awesome than You Think!
"People are more prone to believe the WONDROUSLY FALSE than the WONDROUSLY TRUE."
Charles Mackay

BAR: LOW SELF - CONFIDENCE

Charles Mackay's quote is so true for many of us, and that includes YOU. Yes, I am speaking to you! I am pointing fingers and do you know what is said about a person who points a finger? They have 3 more fingers pointing back at them. So see, I am not being judgmental, I am also included. The bottom line is that many of us - some more than others - focus on the "negative" about ourselves, which most often than not is not true.

We've received messages from others that we internalized and use to govern our lives. As the previous activity showed, we don't have to live our lives by these standards. We have choices. We can change our perspective if we don't want to continue feeling and having the outcomes we are experiencing.

It starts by discerning between what's true and false. The best way to do this is to find actual evidence that support our beliefs -- and when you do find them, you have some choices to make.

SOMETHING TO PONDER
List 6 Wondrously True things about you and evidence of each. Remember, even if a few "not so positive" things come to mind – stop and think. Is this a blessing in disguise? Can I turn this lemon into some refreshing lemonade?

Now it's your turn!

WONDROUS TRUES	EVIDENCE
I inspire people	*I am told on a continuous basis by friends and sometimes strangers that they feel better after talking to me.*
a.	
b.	
c.	
d.	
e.	
f.	

I LEARNED THAT…

_____

_____

_____

Tip: *I'm alright the way I am.*

You're A Gift!
"Life is only traveled once; today's moment becomes tomorrow's memory. Enjoy every moment, good or bad, because *the GIFT of LIFE is LIFE itself.*"

Unknown

BAR: SELF WORTH

According to Merriam-Webster dictionary, the word 'gift' means *something given, talent.* The Encarta Dictionary defines it as *the act of giving something to somebody to provide pleasure or to show gratitude.* 'Gift' as it is being used in this book encompasses all of the above.

- *Something given* - We were born and are alive.

- *Talent* - Each of us have skills, abilities that are unique to each of us.

- *Something given to provide pleasure* - We exist so that we can use our talents to make this world a better place.

- *Something given to show gratitude* - Relationships are critical to living a fulfilling life and healthy relationships involve reciprocity and showing of our appreciation.

If the above is true, we were born to use our unique skills and abilities to make a difference in this world and bring out the best in each other. Then why are so many of us feeling so unfulfilled and unhappy? Some say it's lack of purpose, or how we think, our past, our parents and some will blame anything that comes across their path. The answer to this question is different for each person, and the only person who can answer it is YOU!

For the next 7 days, starting TODAY, write 1 thing that is an indicator that YOU ARE A GIFT.

DAY 1:
DAY 2:
DAY 3:
DAY 4:
DAY 5:
DAY 6:
DAY 7:

I LEARNED THAT…

_____

_____

_____

Tip: *I am a one of a kind gift. There is no one else like me.*

PONDER THIS₇

It's Time to Let Go
"A closed fist cannot receive."
Faith Saunders

BAR: UNCERTAINTY

Try this - fold your hand into a fist. What does it evoke you? For me it makes me feel restricted, tense, angry - I could go on and on. This is how some people go about life and it emits a negative energy.

 Now, try this! Open your hand. What feelings does this evoke in you? I feel relaxed, open, centered, peaceful… A totally different energy - a positive one.

If you had to choose one, who would you prefer to be around? I am guessing the latter – someone who is pleasant and open. Take a few minutes and think about how you're showing up in the world. Of course, we cannot be open and warm all the time, but it is not healthy to be closed most of the time either.

Do you go through life with your hands folded into a fist or are they open to receive? *Explain*

_____

_____

_____

_____

_____

_____

_____

_____

_____

_____

_____

_____

_____

_____

_____

_____

_____

_____

_____

_____

_____

_____

I LEARNED THAT...

_____

_____

Tip: Be mindful of how you're showing up in the world because it impacts how you're treated by others.

PONDER THIS₈

You're Being Remodeled
"I am perfect in my imperfections."
Brene Brown

BAR: PERFECTIONIST

What an oxymoron if I ever heard one. Who we are is a reflection of our life experiences, and our molding started from the second we exited the womb. In other words, this journey called life is not a smooth ride. Each of us has encountered a bump or two (or three or more) in our lifetime. Some bumps have just been anthills. Others seem impossible to get over because they were/are as high as a mountain, and some of us even have scars as a result of them.

I am not sure if you remember your high school science class when you were taught about the life cycle of butterflies? Some of you may remember. I left high school over 30 years ago so, I had to look up the information. One interesting thing I found as I read the description of the metamorphosis process – which means transformation or change in shape in Greek - was that the "pupa stage" (which is the Transition Stage) can last from a few weeks to a month or longer. Some species have a pupa stage that last for two years. *During this time, it may look like nothing is going on but big changes are happening inside.* Special cells that were present in the larva are now growing rapidly. They will become the legs, wings, eyes and other parts of the butterfly.

As with the butterfly, our bumps are preparing us so we can eventually be strong enough to fly away. Each bump serves a purpose as it does in the metamorphosis process, and there is no shortcut around it.

So what are some of the bumps that you have encountered along your life's journey? What lessons did you learn?

BUMPS (Life Experiences)	LESSONS LEARNED

I LEARNED THAT…

_____

_____

_____

Tip: I am perfect with my imperfections.

PONDER THIS$_9$

You're the Lead Actor/Actress in Your Life
"If death meant just leaving the stage long enough to change costume and come back as a new character... Would you slow down? Or speed up?"

Chuck Palahniuk

BAR: LACK OF SELF ACCEPTANCE

I read Chuck Palahniuk's quote and without hesitation knew my answer. Drum roll... *I would slow down.* Ask me this same question two years ago and my reply would've been totally different. I would have the Guinness World record for costume changing. I would slow down today, because I love my life and who I am. I could not say so in the past because I was not comfortable in my own skin.

My belief system was very tainted, and I was always looking at the negative instead of the positive -- comparing myself with others and frankly being a jerk to myself. I now realize that I am the lead actress in my life.

What's your respond to Chuck's question? *Explain*

_____

_____

_____

_____

_____

_____

_____

_____

_____

_____

_____

_____

_____

_____

_____

_____

_____

_____

_____

_____

_____

_____

I LEARNED THAT…

_____

_____

_____

Tip: *Love the one you're with - YOU!*

FEAR: *False Evidence Appearing Real*
"Before you run, check to see if the bulldog has teeth."
Les Brown

BAR: FEAR

The Les Brown quote is funny, but so true. Fear manifests itself in many ways in our lives. For instance, in my case, one of the physical ways that it shows up is as a tight, painful knot in the pit of my stomach. Fear is a very powerful emotion, and it can make a big difference between contentment and regret, success and failure, happiness and sadness. You get the point!

When I looked up the word fear in the dictionary, it was described as *"a very unpleasant or disturbing feeling caused by the presence or imminence of danger."* I will use a personal experience to illustrate. A few years ago I planned a one-day seminar and two weeks before the event, no one registered. To put things into perspective, there was a lot at stake here. Such as loss of a decent amount of money that I paid to the location and the caterer; loss of precious time that was invested in preparing the material and marketing it; my diminished reputation and, of course, my bruised ego.

So now it's all out there; that was what this particular fear was all about, I had some choices to make.

1. I could've remained paralyzed and stuck with my fear. What good would that have done except increase my anxiety and make me feel worst about the situation?
2. Cancel the event and lose my money.
3. I still had 2 weeks before the event. There was time to go back to the drawing board and look at others ways of promoting the event because obviously that what I was doing was not working. There had to be another way!

There are 25 people somewhere who could benefit from this training, and who were willing to pay $99 to attend because they saw value in it. Where were they? How could I demonstrate that what I am offering would add value to their lives?

4. I could have the event for which I paid for anyway, and invite friends and others to attend without charging them. Use the experience to fine tune the seminar and gain feedback.

After evaluating my options, I chose two of them. They were options 3 and 4 above. I filled the unsold seats by inviting a few folks who I knew wanted to attend, but could not afford to do so at the time. It was a win - win for all.

Do you feel trapped between a wall and a bull dog that may not have any teeth? List 3 fears that are holding you hostage?

1. _____

_____

_____

2. _____

_____

_____

3. _____

_____

_____

Choose the most pressing fear from the above list and write 3 possible solutions. Brainstorm with someone – remember – *sometimes 2 heads are better than 1!*

1. _____

_____

_____

_____

_____

2. _____

_____

_____

_____

_____

_____

3. _____

_____

_____

_____

_____

I LEARNED THAT…

_____

_____

_____

Tip: *I am facing my fears and taking control of my life.*

PONDER THIS₁₁

Your Scars Are Your Badge of Honor!
"Never be ashamed of your scars. It simply means that you were stronger than what tried to hurt you."

Unknown

BAR: LACK OF INSIGHT

Some of the most down trodden people I know are also some of the strongest people I know. The BIG problem is that they do not know their strength. I say this because it took considerable strength and determination to survive some of what they have gone through but, they see the scars as weaknesses rather than a symbol of their strength. For instance, I have met people who are in recovery from addiction or have had tragic experiences and I walked away wondering how they could still be alive. But, I am reminded that we all have untapped inner strength that we have yet to use.

Next time that you are experiencing a difficult time - ask yourself, *"Have I been down this path before?"* The situation may be different, but I am confident that you have dealt with challenges before."

Exercise time!

a. Think of a difficult experience you had in the past (*write a brief description*).

_____

_____

_____

_____

_____

_____

b. Who were some of the **people** who supported you during this difficult time, and what did they do that was helpful? (*NOTE: It is important to have people who are positive but also ones who will be honest with you and not only tell you what you want to hear.*)

_____

_____

_____

_____

_____

_____

c. What were some of the **healthy** things that you did to help you cope?

_____

_____

_____

_____

_____

_____

I LEARNED THAT…

_____

_____

_____

Tip: *I am strong because of my scars.*

PONDER THIS$_{12}$

Are You Ready?

"For change to occur, you have to believe that it is POSITIVE and POSSIBLE."

Unknown

BAR: UNCLEAR WHY

Sometimes we give up on our goals because we have not clearly identified what is in it for us. That is our WHY. What is it that we have to gain if we stay the course? This is important because if we don't identify the **positive** outcome of this endeavor AND believe that it is **possible**, more than likely, we will give up when the going gets tough.

This is very important to remember because the bigger your why, the more powerful it will be to pull you through the tough time. My why is to help people all over the world to discover a new future. This is my filter when I am faced with challenges. I ask myself two questions:

- "Will this help others to discover a new future?
- "If so, how can I make this happen?"

1. **Identify a goal that you have been putting off.**

 ____

 ____

 ____

 ____

2. **List the POSITIVE outcomes that you would gain if you accomplished the goal you identified.** *(Be specific about who would benefit and what they would gain).*

 ____

_____

_____

_____

_____

_____

_____

3. List the POSITIVE outcomes to others if you accomplished the goal you identified on the previous page. *(Be specific about who would benefit and what they would gain).*

_____

_____

_____

_____

_____

_____

4. If you believe that it is POSSIBLE - write why you hold the belief that this is possible? *(Give examples to emphasize your points).*

_____

_____

_____

_____

_____

_____

_____

_____

I LEARNED THAT...

_____

_____

_____

Tip: *My WHY is positive and possible!*

PONDER THIS₁₃

Trust Yourself!
"I know God will not give me anything I can't handle. I just wish that he didn't trust me that much."

Mother Teresa

BAR: DOUBT

Do you trust YOURSELF?

This seems to be a straight forward question right? Either you do or you don't! My response is, "It depends."

When I first was asked the question, I responded with a definite 'Yes, if I don't trust myself who will?' But as I took a look at my life's blue print I began to see patterns – inconsistencies in my behavior that told another story.

Closer examination of these patterns showed that I had a tendency to do the things that were easy for me to accomplish, but the more challenging and loftier a goal, the less likely I was to follow through. The reasons varied, but the underlying thread that connected them all was my lack of trust in my ability to be successful; hence, I indulged in self-sabotaging behaviors. This was an eye opener for me.

According to Psychology Today, *"we engage in self-sabotaging behavior to escape intense negative feelings."* In my case, my lack of self-confidence conjured up so much intense negative feelings that my self-sabotaging behavior, procrastination, put obstacles in my path that resulted in me not having to face my fear of failure. In other words, I used these obstacles as the reason for failing.

The games we play! We self-sabotage ourselves in many ways. Procrastination is a major culprit; other examples – comfort eating when we are trying to takeoff weight, going shopping when we are in debt, drinking when we are in recovery, etc. The sad thing is that most of the times, we are not even aware of what we are doing because these self-distractions often do not have immediate consequences.

So… let's talk. As Iyanla Vanzant would say, "Tell the truth!" My truth is that this chapter is self-serving. I was working on a major project and I began to realize that my old friend, procrastination, was showing up frequently. This was my sign that I had to do some self-exploration to see what was really happening. I uncovered that it was my old foe - my fear of failure. Just keeping it real!

PONDER THIS!
What's your blue print? What picture has it painted?

_____

_____

_____

_____

_____

_____

_____

_____

_____

_____

_____

_____

_____

_____

_____

I LEARNED THAT…

_____

_____

_____

Tip: I believe in me!

PONDER THIS[14]

*Stop Focusing on What You Don't Have and
Start Focusing on What You Have*
"Be thankful for what you have; you'll end up having more."
Oprah Winfrey

BAR: FOCUSING ON THE WRONG THING

IF YOU HAVE
*Food in your fridge, clothes on your back, a roof over your
head and a place to sleep*
You're richer than 75% of the world!

IF YOU HAVE
Money in the bank, your wallet, and some spare change
You're among the top 8% of the world's wealthy!

IF YOU
Woke up this morning with more health than illness
***You're more blessed than THE MILLIONS of people
who will not survive this week!***

IF YOU HAVE
*Never experienced the danger of battle
The agony of imprisonment or torture or the horrible pangs of
starvation*
***You're luckier than 500 MILLION people alive and
suffering!***

IF YOU CAN
Read this message
***You are more fortunate than 3 BILLION people in the world
who cannot read at all!***
- Anonymous -

***Tip:** Be grateful for what you have.*

PONDER THIS[15]
What Mask Are You Wearing?
"The privilege of a lifetime is to become who you truly are."
C.G. Jung

BAR: INAUTHENTICITY

"What Mask Are You Wearing?" You may be wondering, *"What is she referring to?"* I have no plans to go to a masquerade party, or it's not Halloween. You are right! I'm referring to how you are showing up in the world. Are you showing up as your authentic self, or do you wear a 'mask' based upon who you are with and/or where you are?

We all wear a mask at some point in our life - some more than others, but frequency does not matter. The fact that we do this is the point of this chapter. Why do we wear masks? Relinquishing your mask(s) means as, Brene Brown puts it, a way of, *"Letting go of who you think you are supposed to be and embrace who you are."*

I can only speak for myself but for a long time I wore various masks because *'I feared that if people really knew me, they would not like me.'* Hence, my need to be liked by others manifested itself in my life in dysfunctional ways. For instance: I didn't know how to say, what many people feel is a bad word – NO! I suffered from *Yes Syndrome*! I did things because I wanted to be liked, even though I felt miserable and resentful while doing it.

I would not speak up and share what I was really thinking and feeling. This often resulted in me walking around feeling upset at myself. (Side bar, when this happens consistently, it can result in depression which is basically anger turned inward.)

I learned that my behavior was FEAR based. Remember what the acronym stands for? *False Evidence Appearing Real*! Well, with much work and some help, I have learned to show up as my authentic self. Do I show up authentically 100% of the time? I would be lying if I said I did. BUT I would say that 80% of the time I do and the other 20% of the time I check myself to see what is happening. It's usually my *inferiority* gremlin playing tricks with me.

When we start showing up as our authentic self, a number of things begin to happen:

- We focus more on how we feel than what other people may think or say.
- We are more contented and at peace with ourselves.
- Other people want to be around us because they sense our true spirit.
- We spend our energy and time with people who truly matters.
- And, of course, there is less drama!

The million dollar question is, *"Why do you wear your mask?"* and the million dollar answer is... *(Only you can fill in the blank)*.

_____

_____

_____

_____

_____

_____

_____

I LEARNED THAT...

_____

_____

_____

Tip: Be authentic – it's easier because no mask is needed.

PONDER THIS₁₆
Culprit BEHIND the Mask
"Shame corrodes the very part of us that believes we are capable of change."

Brené Brown

BAR: SHAME

In the previous chapter I asked the question, ***"What Mask Are You Wearing?"*** Now, I think it is appropriate to talk about one of the main culprits that cause us to wear our masks – **SHAME!**

Everyone has shame about something or another. It is a natural part of the human experience. However, before I go any farther, I think it's important to distinguish between *shame* and *guilt* because sometimes we use them interchangeably and they are different. Brene Brown, in her book *The Gift of Imperfection: Let Go of Who You Think You're Supposed to Be and Embrace Who You Are* describes them best.

- ***SHAME*** *is the intensely painful feeling or experience of believing that we are flawed and therefore unworthy of love and belonging.* Shame is about who you are. Example: I am a bad parent.

- ***GUILT*** *occurs when we hold up something we've done or failed to do against the type of person we want to be.* Guilt is about something that you did. Example: I did not go to my daughter's play because I had to work.

The premise of both is fear of not being loved and connected. Both of which are our strongest needs because we all have a primal need for connection and love. According to Dr. Linda Hartling, the Director of Human Dignity and Humiliation Studies at the Stone Center, when we experience shame, we respond in the following ways.

We move
1. Away from it – withdraw, hide, become silent, keep secrets
2. Towards it – appeasing and pleasing other
3. Against it (gain power over it) – become aggressive and use shame to fight shame

My chosen course of action was always #1, and depends on who I am with and where I was, #2. You'll notice that in most, or all, of my writings I give examples from my personal experience. This wasn't always the case. In the past, I was so ashamed that I would not share aspects of my personal life. However, as I embarked on my "healing journey" I've learned that one way for me to grow and claim my presence in this world is to share - not only the good things, but some of the not so good things because *shame thrives on secrets.* The deeper and darker the secret, and the longer we carry it, the more difficult it is to overcome.

The following are some questions to help you to start mastering your shame.

1. What are you ashamed of?

_____

_____

_____

_____

_____

_____

_____

_____

_____

_____

2. When shame raises its ugly head, what do you do? *Check all that applies and give examples.*

☐ **Move away from it** – withdraw, hide, become silent, keep secrets

_____

_____

_____

_____

_____

_____

_____

_____

_____

☐ **Towards it** – appeasing and pleasing other

_____

_____

_____

_____

_____

_____

_____

_____

_____

_____

_____

☐ **Move against it** (gain power over it) – be aggressive and use shame to fight shame

_____

_____

_____

_____

_____

_____

_____

_____

_____

I LEARNED THAT…

_____

_____

_____

Tip: *I have nothing to be ashamed of.*

You Have No Need to Be Envious
"Someone's victory is not your defeat."
Anonymous

BAR: ENVY

Being authentic means learning to embrace all aspects of one self. Some of these parts we would like to go away but they raise their ugly head periodically. I had one such demon that plagued me occasionally. I called it jealousy, but I later found that it was envy. Although, this emotion can be a great source of pain, it's normal and can give great insight into what we are looking for in our lives.

Envy vs Jealousy

Many people, including myself, use these words interchangeably. The main difference between envy and jealousy is that **ENVY** *is an emotion related to coveting what someone else has.* For example, Joan was envious of her friend who went to Paris on her honeymoon. **JEALOUSY** *is the emotion related to fear that something you have will be taken away by someone else.* For instance, John became jealous when his girlfriend spoke to her high school boyfriend at her ten-year class reunion.

An article in Psychology Today describes envy as basically saying, *"I'm inferior, and I'm hostile."* The article goes on to say, *"When we decide that we're inferior or lack some desirable trait or circumstance - be it beauty, intelligence, spare cash, or an apparently happy marriage - it's normal to feel hostile and focus on our perceived rival's faults and lacks."*

Before I continue, I have to confess that when I had my most recent encounter with envy (can't say my final encounter because I don't know what the future holds) I was so ashamed. I did not want to process my feelings on paper out of fear that someone else might read it. I decided to write what I was feeling and then destroy it. Well, you may be wondering, how did it end up in this book?

The research was helpful. It normalized what I was feeling. It repeatedly mentioned that this is an emotion that people don't speak about. I realized that it would be inauthentic of me not to share my experience. By not doing so, I would continue to give it power. Finally, I believe that sharing this could help someone else face up to one of the demons that maybe holding them back from their greatness.

My Story
A dear friend of mine and I were speaking on the phone. She was sharing some good news about her business. I responded by saying things like, *"I am so happy for you and that is great news"* but my emotions were not matching those words.

This is not a regular occurrence in my life. But when it had happened in the past, I had spent weeks feeling crappy – mostly ashamed and angry at myself. This time I was determined to get to the reason.

The Process
After I realized what I was dealing with, I wanted to figure out what was at the root of this, so I asked myself some questions. The first of which was, **how is this feeling of envy manifesting itself in my life?**

- I did not feel happy for others' good fortune

- There was a mismatch between what was happening on the inside (how I was feeling and thinking) and outside (my actions).

- There was physical pain – I had a subtle pain in my stomach.

- I wasn't sharing information that would help others

- I was celebrating inward when something did not go well for someone.
- I isolated myself because I didn't want to hear about or see the person's good fortune, and I was also feeling ashamed.

Next, I asked myself, **what's behind all of this?** Yes, I now know that feeling inferior was a cause of the problem, but what was I feeling inferior about?

I decided to use the "5 whys" question-asking technique to get to the core of my problem. Basically, it's easy. Each time you get the answer to your question, question it by asking yourself why. Do this 5 times and it helps you to get to the core of the problem.

In my case, I was feeling envy because I had started a new endeavor, and I was not getting the result that I wanted, so I was embarrassed. As I dug deeper, quite a few things came up. Namely, I was not doing the work that was needed to get the results I wanted – networking, strategic planning, and so forth. My friend was. Hence, she was getting results! As I dug deeper, rooted 'issues' came forth. For instance, my age old "headtrash" soundtrack, *"You're not good enough!"* My approaching the situation from a point of scarcity – *there's not enough for everyone.* My focusing on weaknesses instead of strengths. And -- *drum roll* – MY FEAR OF FAILURE!

Lessons Learned

This was quite an experience but one that I will cherish. I found that:

1. Envy is normal. What gives it power over us is the shame that accompanies it.
2. Uncovering the root of your envy can be very liberating because it can provide insight about what you're yearning for in your life.

It's your turn! Remember to tell the truth!

1. **Think about a time that you felt envy, describe the situation?**

   _____

   _____

   _____

   _____

   _____

   _____

2. **How did this make you feel?**

   _____

   _____

   _____

   _____

   _____

   _____

3. **How did it show up in your life?**

   _____

   _____

   _____

   _____

   _____

   _____

4. **Use the 5 WHY Strategy mentioned above to uncover the root of this emotion.**
   WHY #1:_____

_____

_____

_____

WHY #2: _____

_____

_____

_____

WHY #3: _____

_____

_____

_____

WHY #4: _____

_____

_____

_____

WHY #5: _____

_____

_____

_____

_____

I LEARNED THAT…

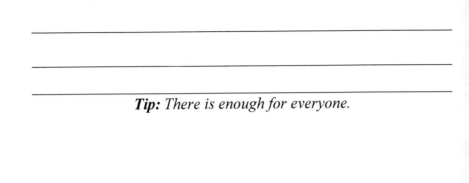

Tip: There is enough for everyone.

PONDER THIS[18]
Your Story Matters
"There is no greater agony than bearing an untold story inside you."
Maya Angelou

BAR: LOW SELF WORTH

Wow! Have you read something that just stopped you in your tracks? Well, that is what happened when I came across that quote by Maya Angelou. It's no wonder so many of us walk around feeling miserable and depressed. Notice that I said *"us."* The *reason being, I know what this pain feels like personally.* Even sadder, many people have been in this place for so long that it has become a normal state of being. It not only impacts them, but their loved ones and others they encounter. What do I mean? When we are in emotional agony it impacts our life in many ways, such as:

Personal Impact
- Unexplained ache and pains
- Agitation and irritability
- Anxiety
- Social isolation
- Substance use including drinking**
- Thinking often about death or wishing to be dead
- Loss of interest in activities the you usually enjoy
- Feeling of hopelessness
- Indecisiveness
- Self-blame
  ** *Drinking is something to pay special attention to because it is socially accepted and can easily become a habit – a way to numb our pain that can get out of control.*

Impact on Others
- We treat others disrespectfully, especially people we love.

- We say hurtful things
- We are not authentic in our interactions. Result, people don't really get to know us.

Why Do We Bury Our Story?

The #1 culprit – SHAME! As was mentioned in PONDER THIS₁₆, Brene Brown defines shame as: *"The intensely painful feeling or experience of believing that we are flawed and therefore unworthy of love and belonging – something we've experienced, done, or failed to do makes us unworthy of connection."*

She goes on to say that for majority of people our **"shame tapes and gremlins keep us feeling *afraid* and *small"*.** Most important, the thing (or things) we are ashamed of was done to us, and is not due to anything that we did ourselves.

There is great value in owning our story.

- **Freedom** -- I call this freedom of the ghost because we are no longer in bondage by something that we or others cannot see or even most important, it is not real. We feel liberated. This means living one's life without fearing what others think and how they will treat us, etc. In addition, it allows us to BE at peace. In other words, as per Brene, *"Only when we are brave enough to explore the darkness will we discover the infinite power of our light."*

- **Liberate Others** -- Marianne Williamson said it best, *"And as we let our own light shine, we unconsciously give other people permission to do the same."*

These are 2 very powerful statements!

What I have found is that the more I own my story and share it, the lighter I feel. In addition, other people's stories help me to have hope. This is empowering by itself. However, for a long time, feeling alone, I kept my story to myself. Like me, many people isolate themselves. We are in silos, living somewhat miserable lives, not realizing that other people have similar stories. Together we can start the healing process.

First Baby Step towards Owning Your Story
Share your story? Face it and tell *yourself* the truth because sometimes in order to numb the pain, we sometimes tell ourselves lies or edit our story.

_____

_____

_____

_____

_____

_____

_____

_____

_____

_____

_____

_____

LEARNED THAT…

_____

_____

_____

Tip: My story is rich - filled with nuggets and clues to shape my and other's future.

PONDER THIS$_{19}$
I Choose To Be Free
"Everybody's got a past. The past does not equal the future unless you live there."
Tony Robbins

BAR: YOUR PAST

FREEING OF THE GHOST
Faith Saunders

Fingers are tingling,
Heart pounding
Sense of excitement in my soul
There is freeing of the ghost!

Minds start racing
GOOD thoughts start swirling
POSITIVE visions are emerging
There is freeing of the ghost!

WILL to live!
NEED to give!
An urge to create is emerging
There is freeing of the ghost!

Now spread your wings wide
Let the Spirit soar free
It's not too late
The ghost is free!

Freeing of the Ghost expresses some of the feeling that emerged when I started to clean out my closet and release *some* of my ghosts (also known as baggage). I say "some" because honestly, I am a work in progress so there will always be work to do. Remember this journey of transformation is a lifetime process that only ends when we die.

Freeing ones ghosts (baggage) takes a lot of energy and most of all, it involves taking on a new *attitude*. Let's face it; some of these ghosts have been my only companions for a long time. I used them as a crutch to justify some of my behaviors. Sometimes they were the only guest at my pity parties and MY only solace during the difficult times. However, they were/are only ghosts. They live in the land of the dead and I am in the land of the living; two different worlds.

Each stanza describes the various emotions that emerged through this transformation process. For instance, *'sense of excitement in my soul'* describes the relief and freedom that I began to feel when I started to open up and let go of some of my secrets; *'positive visions are surfacing'* and *'Will to live! Need to give! An urge to create is emerging'*- describes the lifting of my depression and how I wanted to be a part of life again. The last stanza - describes my utopia; that is, what I think life will be like when I relinquish all of my ghosts.

Relinquishing your ghosts is liberating and as India Arie says in her song *I Choose*:

> *I done been through some painful things*
> *I thought that I would never make it through.*
> *Filled up with shame from the top of my head*
> *to the soles of my shoes.*
> *I put myself in so many chaotic circumstances,*
> *But by the grace of God I've been given*
> *so many second chances.*
> *But today I decided to let it all go.*
> *I'm dropping these bags,*
> *I'm making room for my joy.*

Learn from your past:

1. Do you have "ghosts" (baggage) that are haunting you (holding you back)?   YES   NO

2. If you answered YES to question 1 - what are they?

_____

_____

_____

_____

_____

_____

_____

_____

_____

3. How are they manifesting themselves in your life?

_____

_____

_____

_____

_____

_____

_____

_____

4. If you answered NO to question 1 - What was the turning point in your life when you decided that you had to release your ghost?

_____

_____

_____

_____

_____

_____

_____

_____

5. How did you go about freeing them?

_____

_____

_____

_____

_____

_____

6. What are some of the changes that have occurred in your life since you have released your ghosts?

_____

_____

_____

_____

_____

_____

_____

I LEARNED THAT…

_____

_____

Tip: _"Everybody's got a 'thing'. Some 'things' are nice and quiet._
Some 'things' have fangs and claws. Some 'things' stink and have
slobber everywhere."
Iyanla Vanzant

YOU HAVE TO

BE

BEFORE YOU CAN DO,

DO

BEFORE YOU CAN

HAVE

Zig Ziglar

PONDER THIS$_{20}$

Struggling Is Necessary In Order to Grow
"Sometimes you have to be in a struggle to fix a struggle."
Maalum Moja

BAR: CONFLICT

I distinctly remember when I first heard someone say the above quote by Maalum Moja – *"Sometimes you have to be in a struggle to fix a struggle."* At the time I heard it, it took my breath away because I had a profound "aha" moment.

Background: At the time I heard this quote I was going through a deep depression. I was at a point in my life where I was questioning my purpose, although at the time I had no clue that was the cause of my discomfort. All I knew was that I felt really lousy.

On the outside, my life looked peachy. Honestly, I should have been happy, but it was quite the opposite and that was part of the problem. I felt ungrateful for feeling the way I was feeling.

Have things in your life ever been so bad that you felt there were only two ways out? One of them was not an option for me, so I had to do the work. I call this my "valley" experience. When I'd originally thought about a valley, I envisioned a cold and dark place. However, I have discovered that the land at the bottom of a valley can be very fertile, which makes it excellent for farming. Hence, my valley experience helped me to grow considerably because I did a lot of introspective soul searching there.

Have you ever procrastinated about completing a task due to fear or self-doubt? Sound familiar? Hint: prison cells! This was the source of my pain. I knew what I was supposed to be doing with my life, but I was held hostage by my cells of fear, self-doubt, etc.

It took me a while to really break free. A number of times I was released. I'd do what I had to do for a while, but then I would relapse into my old ways and slip back into my depressive state. Today I am happy to say that I feel truly liberated because I did the work.

You may be wondering why I repeatedly refer to, "doing the work." Sorry to say, there are no freebies here. You have to work on your stuff so that you can break free. Here are some of the work activities that I did to break free.

1. **Paid attention to how I was feeling and the associated thought patterns**

   I tracked this on a daily basis. Did I do it consistently? Definitely not! However, I did it enough so that I soon realized patterns. For instance, I realized that when I was in certain situations and around certain people, my mood changed -- sometimes for the better and in others for the worst.

2. **Faced the fact that I was responsible to get out of my rut and that I had choices - accept the status quo or do something about it.**

   Each of us is responsible for our life. I strongly believe that each of us is given an assignment and we received the gifts and talents to perform it while we are on this earth. However, like me, many are stuck in their valley because they are not taking responsibility to complete their assignment.

3. **Acknowledged I didn't have to travel the journey alone and – GOT HELP!**

   I solicited help from others who I trusted and knew that they would be honest and hold me accountable. That was a critical step for two reasons:

a. When you are in this space emotionally and physically, one part of you wants to feel better while another part just wants to keep things status quo.

b. Going solo without support is a recipe for failure!

I went back to therapy to get help to uncover what was happening to me. While I am encouraging you to tell the truth – to be authentic -- I have to come clean also. I even went back to taking medication for the depression and I am happy that I did. There is a saying in Jamaica – *"Who feels it knows it!"* In other words, "If you have not been through it, you don't really understand it."

Many people frown upon going for therapy -- especially my people from the Caribbean. But I know firsthand that therapy and medication are nothing to be ashamed of. Case in point, if I were having symptoms of high blood pressure -- I would not skip a beat before I went to the doctor, and I would happily take the medication that was prescribed. In addition, I would not be ashamed to share that information with anyone. However, for some reason mental health challenges have so much stigma associated with them that we are ashamed of sharing that we are not doing well emotionally and/or get help.

4. **Create a plan.**
   I had my friend help me to create an action plan because it was not easy for me to do. Not only that, but it was something that part of me did not want to do. My plan included, journaling daily, doing my devotion, speaking to my support person at least 1 time per day and being honest about what was happening with me. I added other things as I began to feel better.

5. **Kept myself grounded by focusing on the things I was grateful for.**

Over the course of a month I committed to write 100 things that I was grateful for. That might sound easy, but after a while I started running out of things. So I wrote about how grateful I was that I could bend my fingers. It may sound weird, but if you've ever had a cut on one of your fingers and you weren't able to use it, you know how difficult it is to do things with just one finger that is not functioning.

6. **Gave myself grace**

   Things don't always go as we planned. Giving myself grace was all about letting things go and forgiving myself. My friend helped me to stay focused on what went well instead of dwelling on the negative.

   It is very important to **consciously** acknowledge and write down what helped us through our valley experience because it won't be the last time we'll travel that path. It's equally important to note what did NOT work so we don't reinvent dysfunctional patterns.

What have been some indicators that you were in a valley experience?

_____

_____

_____

_____

_____

_____

_____

_____

_____

_____

_____

_____

_____

_____

What are some of the things that you did to feel better?

_____

_____

_____

_____

_____

_____

_____

_____

_____

I LEARNED THAT…

_____

_____

_____

Tip: *"Where there is no struggle, there is no strength."*
Oprah Winfrey

PONDER THIS₂₁

Tick Tock, Tick Tock - Time Is Going
"How did it get so late so soon?"
Dr. Seuss

BAR: TIME

Below is a diagram which provides a visual of the activity that will be described next.

1. Stand between two walls. Imagine that you are standing on a straight line which starts from the left wall and goes across the room to the right wall. This line represents time. The left wall represents your birth date, and the one on your right represents that unknown day in the future when you take your last breath. I know, death is one topic many of us don't want to think about. Yet, talk about it or not, it is inevitable. For the purpose of this exercise, let's assume that you're going to live to be 100 years old. My prayer is that it will be longer.

2. Estimate a point on the invisible line that represent your current age and stand at that spot.

3. In a previous exercise, you identified what you would be doing with your life if you had no limitations. Close your eyes and envision some of the things you wrote you would like to accomplish. **While doing so, take small baby steps going towards the right wall.**

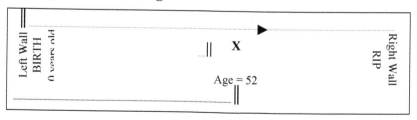

What were your thoughts when you did the exercise?

_____

_____

_____

_____

_____

_____

_____

_____

_____

How did you feel?

_____

_____

_____

_____

_____

_____

_____

I LEARNED THAT…

_____

_____

_____

Tip: *Time waits for no (wo)man. It does not stop while we are thinking about the things we would like to do.*

MINDfield
"I myself am the *enemy* who must be loved."
Carl Jung

BAR: FAULTY THINKING

Now that you have established that you are a fabulous person who has a lot going on, let's take a few minutes to explore where we get some of our negativity from. I won't go into a whole lecture of how the brain is structured and so forth – BORING and honestly, that is not my area of expertise! Instead, I would like to emphasize that the enemy is not outside. Although people talk about haters, personally I don't buy into that, but that's a discussion for another book.

Your strongest and most destructive enemy is you! Yes! Once again I am pointing fingers. I am not going to tell you anything you don't already know, but the mass that lies between our ears is a very powerful resource or it can be a lethal weapon. I am speaking about our minds. At times we use our mind as a weapon against ourselves. Face it, if we loved our self unconditionally, we would not say some of the mean things that we continually say to ourselves.

Exercise time! Only, I am not referencing your physical body this time. I am talking about your mind. By the way, both mind and body are related, and we will touch on this later but for now – let's focus on your mind.

Think of someone or something that you love deeply – it could be your child(ren), a significant other, parent, sibling, pet - you choose. List briefly, 3 examples of things that you have said to that person/pet that shows them that you care about them deeply. While doing so - reflect on how you felt, your

tone, pitch and body language when you spoke to them.

a. _____

_____

_____

_____

_____

_____

_____

b. _____

_____

_____

_____

_____

_____

c. _____

_____

_____

_____

_____

_____

Think about some recent conversations that you have had with yourself. Again, list briefly, 3 examples of the things that you have said to yourself. While doing so - reflect on how you felt, your tone and pitch when you spoke to yourself.

a. _____
_____
_____
_____
_____
_____
_____
_____

b. _____
_____
_____
_____
_____
_____
_____

c. _____
_____
_____
_____
_____
_____

I LEARNED THAT...

_____

_____

_____

Tip: _Be kind to yourself._

What Seeds Are You Planting?
**"Our lives will bear the fruit of the seeds we
plant in our minds."**
Iyanla Vanzant

BAR: PLANTING WEEDS

This quote by Iyanla Vanzant is very powerful. It ties in perfectly with the quote from Carl Jung in the previous chapter. Based upon your response to the previous Ponder This activity – what seeds (thoughts) would you say that you are planting on a regular basis? Will they bring forth roses or weeds?

Another way of assessing what seeds you have planted (or are planting) is to examine your life. My only word of caution is, as Iyanla would say is, *"Tell the truth!"*

1.   On a scale of 1 – 5 gauge how have you been feeling about your life within the past 3 months?

Extremely Miserable	Somewhat Miserable	Okay	Somewhat Satisfied	Extremely Satisfied

2.   Describe in details your feelings.

_____

_____

_____

_____

_____

_____

_____

_____

3. Have any life changes - birth/death, marriage, divorce, separation, change in work situation and so forth - contributed to the way you have been feeling?

     YES   **NO** (*If YES, explain what it is?*)

_____

_____

_____

_____

_____

_____

_____

_____

4. If you answered 1, 2 or 3 on the scale, list two things that you will do within the next 24 hours to make you feel better?

_____

_____

_____

_____

_____

_____

_____

_____

_____

_____

_____

_____

_____

_____

_____

_____

_____

5. If your answered 4 or 5 on the scale, list 2 things that you will do to keep this momentum going?

_____

_____

_____

_____

_____

_____

_____

_____

_____

_____

_____

_____

_____

_____

_____

I LEARNED THAT...

_____

_____

_____

Tip: *I have control over how I think and feel!*

Move Forward
"Let the healing begin!"
Faith Saunders

BAR: PAST HURTS

Earlier, you did an exercise that demonstrated that time waits for none of us. It does not stop. I cannot tell you how much time I have wasted thinking about what happened to me in the past. Countless hours ruminating about what he/she said and did. While doing so, I am getting angry and sometimes so upset that I begin to cry. The bizarre thing is that the person I was upset with had no clue that I am holding on to stuff. They are out living their life. Does this make any sense? On the surface, might not, but our feeling don't lie. They are an indicator that we have work to do.

So how do we move forward from the hurt? Drum roll... FORGIVENESS! So what does it mean to forgive?

> Psychologists defines **forgiveness** as a ***conscious, deliberate*** decision to **release** *feelings of resentment or vengeance toward a person or group who has* **harmed** *you, although they may not deserve your forgiveness.*

I agree with this definition for the most part, but I feel that it left out one very important factor. That factor is that many times the person that we have to forgive is **our self**! I mentioned earlier that I spent time thinking about my past. Well, a large part of my anger was towards myself. What I did or didn't do when the incident occurred.

Now, let's dissect the above definition so that we are all on the same page. Forgiveness is a ***conscious*** act. This is critical! I solicited the help of "Mr. Webster Dictionary" to help me with this. According to the dictionary - conscious means *to be aware of something (such as a fact or feeling: knowing that something exists or is happening* (or happened). Hence, **the first step in our forgiveness journey is acknowledging that we are hurting.**

Next, we have to make a ***deliberate*** decision. Once again, Webster came to the rescue. The word deliberate means *to think about or discuss issues and decisions carefully.* Hence, **the second step in our forgiveness journey has many parts.**

- Think about what occurred in an objective way or
- Discuss the situation with someone you trust and who will be honest with you. I think this is very important because sometimes we are so close to a situation that we cannot separate the forest from the trees.
- Make a decision about what you are going to do.

As per the definition, we have to ***release*** the feelings that are holding us hostage. This is easier said than done! Therefore, it is the most difficult of the three steps.

So how do we release? Releasing does not mean glossing over or denying the seriousness of the situation; nor does it mean forgetting, condoning or excusing what occurred. The jury is out on this one, but it doesn't mean that you have to reconcile with the person. When we forgive, we have peace of mind and we are free from deeply held negative feelings. Hence, **the third and very important step is *releasing* the feeling of resentment and vengeance toward the person, group or yourself.** In other words, thoughts about them, or even seeing them, does not bring emotional pain.

PONDER THIS!
1. Who do you have to forgive?

_____

_____

_____

_____

_____

_____

2. **In 3 sentences, describe what the person or group did that hurt you?**

_____

_____

_____

_____

_____

_____

_____

_____

3. **How has this hurt impacting your life?** Remember, *tell the truth!*

_____

_____

_____

_____

_____

_____

_____

_____

_____

4. What are you willing to do to free YOURSELF from this emotional pain?

_____

_____

_____

_____

_____

_____

_____

_____

_____

_____

_____

I LEARNED THAT…

_____

_____

_____

Tip: *You have to let go of the hurt and pain … to receive what's in store for your life.*

PONDER THIS$_{25}$
Defeating Yourself
"Some people create their own storms, and then get upset when it rains!"
Unknown

BAR: SELF SABOTAGE

WOW! I almost fell off of my chair when I came across this quote. It's so true. Before going any further, to ensure that we are all on the same page, let's define what self-sabotage means. According to Margaret Paul, Ph.D., bestselling author and relationship expert, *"self-sabotage is a defense response activated by fear and goes into action to try to protect us from getting hurt."*

When we self-sabotage we think and behave in ways that cause us to self-destruct. For instance, we doubt our abilities, undermine our goals and become paranoid about our self and others. The following are other examples of self-sabotaging behaviors.

-   Staying in a job that you hate
-   Being in an unhealthy relationship
-   Doing too much for others and getting angry when they do not reciprocate
-   Getting intimate too early in a relationship and getting angry when the relationship does not work out
-   Starting things but not completing them
-   Procrastination
-   Not delegating
-   Doing things that create debt and other negative consequences
-   Not doing positive things based upon what others may say or think
-   Self-medicating with drugs or alcohol
-   Comfort eating: using food to fill a void or numb

emotional pain
- Engaging in self-injury behaviors such as cutting
- Thinking and speaking meanly to one's self
- Eating unhealthy food
- Staying up late when you're tired

Can you relate to any of the above? The sad thing is that, many people don't realize that their behaviors are self-sabotaging. Simple example, Mary had a great week and she wants to treat herself. What did she decide to do? She went shopping! Guess what? Mary has debt collectors stressing her out on a daily basis because she cannot pay her bills. Is she nurturing herself or causing harm? Do you know someone like Mary? Or, can you relate to her? There are many ways that Mary could treat herself that cost nothing such as, taking a long, and well deserved, candlelight bubble bath.

So you may be wondering, how do I regain control over these self-defeating thoughts and behaviors?

a. **To solve any problem one has to own the problem. That is, see the problem for what it is and take full responsibility. Write examples of some of the ways that you self-sabotage. Choose from the above list and/or add your own below.**

_____

_____

_____

_____

_____

_____

_____

_____

_____

_____

_____

_____

b. **Explore what the root of your self-sabotaging thoughts and behaviors are. It could go as far back as childhood. You may need someone, like a professional, to help you.**

_____

_____

_____

_____

_____

_____

_____

_____

_____

_____

_____

_____

_____

_____

_____

_____

_____

_____

_____

c. **Below, write a healthy action you will take to combat your most self-destructive self-sabotaging behavior. Remember, to turn any action into a habit, studies show that it takes an average of 66 days to make this change.**

I will *(insert healthy behavior)* _____

_____

instead *of (insert self-sabotaging behavior)* _____

_____

d. **Next, get a regular calendar or your phone calendar - whatever works for you, and start tracking each time you substitute the new healthy behavior for the old one. Do something HEALTHY and NON SELF-DESTRUCTIVE every time you do the new behavior 10 times. This is important because it provides you with small milestones which are less overwhelming to reach.**

I LEARNED THAT...

_____

_____

_____

Tip: *Create your own sunshine and relax in your garden!*

PONDER THIS$_{26}$

Attitude Is Everything!

"It is our attitude toward life that determines life's attitude toward us. We get back what we put out."

Earl Nightingale

BAR: NEGATIVE ATTITUDE

Life is full of challenges - that is why it is worth living! Can you imagine a life without challenges? I don't even want to try. They are what help us to grow and reach our fullest potential. It's our attitude towards these challenges that make a difference. When was the last time you measured your attitude. Maybe it is time to do so because you may need an attitude adjustment! A slight adjustment could make a world of a difference between a POSITIVE or NEGATIVE outcome!

The following are just a few more morsels of wisdom from Earl Nightingale's book – *Lead the Field.* **Choose one that appeals to you and post it where you can see it on a regular basis. Use it to remind you that ATTITUDE IS EVERYTHING!**

1. "Each of us creates his or her own life largely by our attitude."

2. "You can control your attitude. Set it each morning."
3. "Gratitude and expectancy are the best attitude."
4. "Others treat us as we treat them. They react to us. They only give us back a reflection of our own attitude."
5. "Don't wait for change. You change."
6. "People don't have great attitudes because of great success; they have great success largely because of great attitudes."
7. Other *(write your own):*

_____

_____

_____

_____

_____

_____

Which one did you choose and why did you choose it?

_____

_____

_____

_____

_____

_____

_____

_____

_____

_____

I LEARNED THAT…

_____

_____

_____

Tip: I CHOOSE to have a POSITIVE attitude today!

PONDER THIS[27]
Awaken the Sleeping Giant!
"Follow the omens, they are the clues to your future."
Unknown

BAR: INATTENTION

The following are five tips to help you become more self-aware so that you can get a better understanding of what makes you tick. They involve introspection, observation of your behaviors and communicating with others. Write your response in the space below each section.

TIP #1: What makes you excited and energized?

I was speaking with a dear friend recently and she shared that she was questioning her purpose (my words, not hers). She loves what she does professionally, but she feels such happiness when she is able to help others. She said that she wished she could do more community-based work where she could be hands-on helping people. *What my friend is feeling is a big tip to help her gain insight into her gifts/talents and purpose.* What I suggested to her and now to you is to explore these clues. In my friend's case, I suggested that she schedule some volunteer time and pay attention to her thoughts and feelings while doing so.

_____

_____

_____

_____

_____

_____

_____

_____

TIP #2: What do people usually compliment you on?

In other words, what do people often tell you that you are good at? How do you feel when you are doing this? Do you feel elated?

_____

_____

_____

_____

_____

_____

_____

TIP #3: When was the last time you lost track of time?

Are there activities that you get so absorbed in that you don't think about time, or eating, or sleeping when you are doing them? This is a key tip. These could be hobbies and/or leisure activities. They could also be work related.

_____

_____

_____

_____

_____

_____

_____

TIP #4: 'Back in the day' what did you enjoy doing?

Think about when you were growing up. How did you spend your time as a child? What did you like to do? When I was going through my "exploration" phase (this is what I call what we are doing right now), I asked my sister what she remembered about me when I was growing up. One of the things she said was that I was always writing. I did not remember that but I do love writing.

_____

_____

_____

_____

_____

_____

_____

_____

_____

_____

_____

_____

_____

_____

_____

_____

TIP #5: Ask others

As I mentioned previously, my sister gave me great insight. Ask friends, family, colleagues and other people who you trust, one or all of the following questions. This can be extremely helpful because they are able to observe you in a way that you cannot observe yourself. Their input can reveal things that you weren't aware of.

- What makes me unique?
- What do you think I do very well?
- What are my strongest skills?

_____

_____

_____

_____

_____

_____

_____

I LEARNED THAT…

_____

_____

_____

Tip: *I am curious to know what I will uncover today.*

Baby Steps Does It
"You must eat the elephant one bite at a time."

Twi Proverb

BAR: UNREALISTIC GOALS

Everything has a beginning, middle and an end. No matter what the situation, we cannot get to the end without the other two. In positive situations we become excited and rush through the steps, missing one or two *(sound familiar?),* because we want to see the outcome. In unpleasant situations, we rush through because we want it to end quickly. Despite the situation, positive or negative, we have to go through a **PROCESS and TRUST IT!**

For a long time, this book was my elephant. Each time I thought or attempted to write it I got overwhelmed. I finally realized that it was overwhelming because of how I was thinking of it. I love to write, but I was looking at this book not as a means of sharing some of my thoughts with others using my love of writing, but as a project – something that had to be perfect! Once I was able to change my thought process, my attitude also changed and I did not feel pressured. I decided to eat my elephant one bite at a time by writing 1 chapter a day – as you can see each chapter is only a few pages long. This was not only manageable but liberating. Also, I hope this will motivate you to use it!

If we are going through life in a rush to get from point A to Z, there are so many letters that we may miss along the way. All of which, together, makes up the alphabet. In addition, we sometimes get overwhelmed to the point that we become counter-productive. Slowing down and taking small bites have many benefits. Some of which are:
- It helps you to relax and enjoy what you are doing.

- You're more likely to learn new things that can enhance your life.
- It opens up opportunities that you would otherwise miss
- It enhance the quality of your interactions and relationships

Maybe, just maybe, it is time for you to slow down and begin to eat your elephant one bite at a time.

1. **Identify the ELEPHANT in your life?**

_____

_____

_____

_____

_____

_____

_____

_____

_____

_____

_____

_____

_____

_____

_____

_____

_____

2. **What benefits do you see happening for you as you slow down and begin to eat your elephant one bite at a time?**

_____

_____

_____

_____

_____

_____

_____

_____

_____

_____

_____

_____

_____

_____

_____

_____

_____

_____

_____

_____

3. **List 3 small bites that you can take of your elephant within the next 5 days?**

a. _____

_____

_____

_____

b. _____

_____

_____

_____

c. _____

_____

_____

_____

I LEARNED THAT…

_____

_____

_____

Tip: I am taking one bite at a time.

PONDER THIS₂₉

Tunnel Vision
**"Faith is taking the first step even when you don't
see the staircase."**
Martin Luther King, Jr.

BAR: ALL OR NOTHING THINKING

If you have driven in New York City or any major city, I think you can relate to this. It's a beautiful summer day, not too hot and there is a nice breeze. There are people milling around everywhere. As a driver, it can be very difficult to be aware of everything so you don't hit someone or be run over if you are a pedestrian. The good news is that the visibility is clear; therefore, you have a full view of what is happening so you can make informed choices.

The challenge is that in life, things are not as clear cut. Many

times, our view is tainted by many things. Some are physical and others psychological. As a result, we are waiting on the side-lines for everything to become perfect before we start to pursue what we want to manifest in our lives. Sorry to say my friend - many of us have a long wait. Or even worst, the day never comes and we look back at our life with regret. So what are you waiting for?

Dr. King's quote is challenging us to take risks. This is gathering as much information that we can so we can make an intelligent decision and take action. Even with the best information, we sometimes make decisions that do not yield the outcome we expected. But doing something is better than doing nothing.

Remember, that you won't make the right decision all the time and that is okay! As Andy Andrew says in his book, *The Traveler's Gift* - *"God did not give me the ability to always make right decisions. He did, however, give me the ability to make a decision and then make it right."*

1. **Today, take 1 small calculated risk. What will it be?**

_____

_____

_____

_____

_____

_____

_____

_____

2. **When will you do it?**

_____

_____

_____

_____

_____

_____

3. **Where will you do it?**

_____

_____

_____

_____

4. How will you do it?

_____

_____

_____

_____

_____

_____

5. You made your decision and have a plan, what does it feels like?

*BEFORE*_____

_____

_____

_____

_____

_____

_____

_____

6. You did it! *Write what you actually did.*

_____

_____

_____

_____

_____

_____

_____

_____

_____

_____

7. How do you feel?

　　*AFTER*_____

　　_____

　　_____

　　_____

　　_____

　　_____

　　_____

I LEARNED THAT…

_____

_____

_____

Tip: *Keep moving although the path is not clear!*

Stop Making Excuses!
"A life without any goals is like being on a treadmill going nowhere."
Unknown

BAR: EXCUSES

Have you ever had a dream where you have been going somewhere but you cannot seem to get there? I have! And it is one nightmare that I pray that I never have again. I work up sweating, frustrated and honestly scared!

This is a perfect example of some people's lives. They have a JOB that they hate, and there are things that they would like to do, but for whatever reason they don't do anything. Many times the reason is a reasonable one like family obligations and so forth, and sacrifices have to be made. However, it takes a whole lot of energy to go somewhere on a daily basis that you don't want to be, or doing a job you don't like doing. The same relates to relationships and other aspects of your life that is causing you misery.

Eventually, the reason becomes, *I am too old.* Well, I have news for you and Nola Ochs says it best, *"I don't dwell on my age. It might limit what I can do. As long as I have my mind and health, age is just a number."*

Nola holds the Guinness record as the world's oldest college graduate at age 95. She was born in 1911 in Illinois. She graduated high school in 1929 and began college via correspondence course from Fort Hays State University in Kansas. After passing her teacher's certification exam, she taught in county schools for four years before marrying her husband, Vernon Ochs. Soon, the realities of farming sidetracked any thoughts of furthering her education, though Nola lived a good, full life on the farm, raising four sons. She always yearned to learn more about the world she lived in, but not until after Vernon died in 1972 did Nola consider resuming her formal education. In 1988, at age 77, Nola received her associate degree from Dodge City Community College. Long story short - Nola returned to school and at 95 years old she graduated with her bachelor's degree and a 3.7 GPA. Wait, the story did not end there - in May 2010, at age 98, Nola Ochs received her master's degree, making her the oldest person to receive that distinction.

The moral of this story is that you're as old as you feel. You can accomplish what you put your mind to. It may take longer or a little more aches and pains but if you are determine - YOU CAN.

1. **If you were given an opportunity to do 1 thing (with no constraints) what would you do?**

2. **What is getting in the way?**

_____

_____

_____

I LEARNED THAT...

_____

_____

_____

_____

Tip: *While there is a will there is a way!*

PONDER THIS[31]

Life Is Not A Bed of Roses

"Our happiness is certainly mixed in with the tragedies of life. You have to find the lemonade."

Chandra Wilson

BAR: SELF PITY

Have you felt that everything is falling apart in your life and out of the blue you speak with someone or come across something that changes your mindset from gloom to gratitude? This is what happened when I came across the following article by Kiara Kharpertian, *From Infusion to the Aisle: A Bride Plans Her Wedding During Cancer Treatment,* on the Dana Farber Cancer Institute web site.

Kiara wrote, *"The fall season is sort of strange for me. Over the past few years, a number of important things happened during this season. In early October 2010, I was diagnosed with stage III breast cancer at the age of 25. Though I was re-diagnosed stage IV in March 2013, by October 2013, exactly three years to the day that I found that original lump, my scans came back clean – no evidence of disease." But six weeks later, in November 2013, an MRI revealed about a dozen small, scattered brain tumors."*

I could not help but stop to wonder what I would do if I was in Kiara position. My first response was to think, "I could not handle it." However, as I read further, this young lady's courage and zest for life really touched me and helped me to see that a positive attitude, determination and persistence can work miracles.

On October 3, 2014, exactly four years from her original discovery that she had cancer, she was walking down the aisle to join her now husband. She describes planning her wedding while going through a new clinical trial as she continue to "wage war" against

her brain tumors. In addition, she continues to pursue her doctorate studies full time at the English Department at Boston College.
Full Story: *http://blog.dana-farber.org/insight/2014/11/from-infusion-to-the-aisle-a-bride-plans-her-wedding-during-cancer-treatment/*

I learned a lot from this article. You may get something else. The point is that there is a lesson to be learned from everyone's journey.

1. Life throws us curb balls. This is a normal part of the human experience. However, we have choices on how to deal with them. We can face them and deal with them or deny their existence. The choice we make depends upon our attitude. In the above mentioned article, despite all that Kiara was experiencing she had a positive attitude.
2. Time is precious so use it wisely. Kiara is living life to the fullest despite her challenges.
3. Normalizing our given challenges make them easier to face.
4. Someone who truly love us will stand with us through the tough times.
5. To remember to count our blessings! There is at least one in every situation.

Think of a challenging situation that you have encountered. What made it most difficult?

_____

_____

_____

_____

_____

_____

_____
_____
_____
_____

Looking back, what would you have done differently?

_____
_____
_____
_____
_____
_____
_____
_____
_____

I LEARNED THAT…

_____
_____
_____

Tip: *I am ready and open for change.*

Own Your Power

"The moment that we relinquish *our power* to please another, we *disempower* them as well."

Daily Om

BAR: POWERLESSNESS

What I love about the above quote is that it is strength based. Why do we, especially women, have such a desire to please others even when we are hurting ourselves in the process? The reason will vary from one person to another but in my opinion it is the need to be liked. We don't want to hurt others. Questions, is it okay to hurt yourself? Don't your feelings matter? Even more important - Don't YOU matter?

Wait, I envision some of you thinking, *"Putting my feelings above others is selfish."* It depends upon your motive! If you are doing something for someone because you want to do it and it brings you joy to do so, that is one thing. However, if we are doing something and we don't want to do it, but we're just doing it to please the other person, then our motives are not pure. Hence, *we are giving away our power!* That is, exchanging our need to be liked for doing something that we don't want to do.

We are disempowering others when we do things just to be liked, or to please others. We are deceiving them by not being genuine and truthful. In addition, it's disempowering for the person if we're only doing it for them because we feel that they cannot do it good enough, or they'll take too long to do it -- or whatever our reason. By not taking the time to teach them or encourage them to be self-sufficient, our behavior is disempowering and disrespectful. Our actions are showing that we don't believe in them.

One other important point - sometimes we may need to do something that we don't want to do because it truly is helping the person. For instance, my friend was ill and she needed someone to take her to the doctor. When this happened, I had an important meeting that I had to attend -- one that took quite a while to schedule. Honestly, I really did not want to cancel the meeting, but I knew that my friend needed me so I took her to the doctor and cancelled the meeting. It all goes back to motive -- my friend needed me so despite the inconvenience, her wellbeing was most important.

So how do we get out of this cycle? Use the following to help you answer these questions. Don't forget that you bring something of value to your relationships, and that relationships are about reciprocity.

1. **How does it feel when you ignore your feelings to please someone else?**

_____

_____

_____

_____

_____

2. **Identify your motives:** Ask yourself why you are doing this in the first place. In other words, ask yourself the *WIIIFM– What Is In It For Me* question.

_____

_____

_____

_____

_____

_____

_____

3. **If the answer is that you want to be liked, then ask yourself - why is it so important for this individual or group of individuals to like me?**

_____

_____

_____

_____

_____

_____

4. **What would be the likely outcome if I said no the next time I am asked to do something and I don't want to do it?**
    a. Identify the best possible outcome?

_____

_____

_____

_____

_____

_____

    b. Identify the worst possible outcome?

_____

_____

_____

_____

_____

_____

_____

c. What would be the short term implications to you and them?

_____

_____

_____

_____

d. What would be the long term implications to you and them?

_____

_____

_____

_____

e. Could you live with the outcome?

_____

_____

_____

_____

I LEARNED THAT...

_____

_____

_____

Tip: *My thoughts and feelings are as important as someone elses!*

Success Only Comes When You Take Risks!
"Progress always involves risks. You can't steal second base and keep your foot on first."
Fredrick B. Wilcox

BAR: RISK AVERSION

Change is one of the most difficult things for humans to readily accept, although it is a part of the human experience. Can you imagine if we remained an infant all of our lives? The world would not exist for many reasons. First and foremost - there would not be anyone to procreate. Even if this were possible, we would lack the knowledge and wisdom to nurture our young ones. As we grow physically, we acquire certain knowledge and wisdom that helps us and others along our life's journey.

So why is change so difficult for us? Indulge me for a few minutes and do the following exercise. It should take 5 minutes tops!

Activity: Cross YOUR Arms[1]
    a. Stand up and cross your arms - the same way you would if you were upset or waiting for something.
    b. Next fold your arms the other way; that is, the reverse of what you did earlier.

Questions
1. **How did it feel when you cross your arms the first time?**

_____

_____

_____

_____

_____

2. **How did it feel when you were asked to fold your arms the other way? Did it come naturally or did you have to stop and think about it?**

_____

_____

_____

_____

_____

3. **How comfortable were you doing this differently from your normal way? What emotions were you feeling?**

_____

_____

_____

_____

_____

This exercise, demonstrates why many of us avoid change or find it difficult to embrace change. It takes us outside of our comfort zone and forces us to do things that are not familiar and for which we don't know the outcome. However, for us to grow and experience new and exciting things in life we have to be willing to take the risk and leave first base.

I LEARNED THAT…

_____

_____

_____

Tip: I am willing to embrace change so that I can grow

[1]Adapted and modified from http://www.isixsigma.com.

PONDER THIS[34]

Let Go of the Old and Embrace the New!
"Every beginning is a consequence.
Every beginning ends something."

Paul Valery

BAR: FEAR OF CHANGE

Ever wondered why change is so difficult? According to William Bridges in his book *Managing Transition*[2], change is easy, it is transitioning that is hard. He goes on to say that **change is situational**. For instance, if I was once 160 pounds and now I am 130 pounds. I lost 30 pounds. The real challenge was everything in between! In order to lose the weight I had to eat healthier and more frequently, drink water, exercise, reprogram some of my negative thoughts and beliefs and so forth. This is known as the **transition process -** everything that I had to do to lose the weight.

Marilyn Ferguson said it best, *"It's not so much that we're afraid of change or so in love with the old ways, but it's that place in between that we fear... It's like being between trapezes. It's Linus when his blanket is in the dryer. There is nothing to hold on to."*

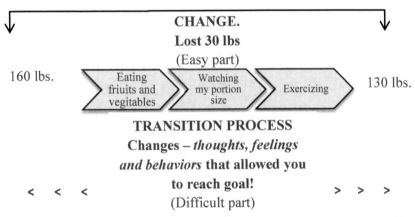

CHANGE.
Lost 30 lbs
(Easy part)

160 lbs.   Eating friuits and vegitables   Watching my portion size   Exercizing   130 lbs.

TRANSITION PROCESS
Changes – *thoughts, feelings*
and behaviors **that allowed you**
to reach goal!
(Difficult part)

1. **Identify a change that you would like to make in your life.**
   Be as specific as you can.

_____

_____

_____

_____

_____

2. **List some of the challenges that you will have to make to reach your goal?**

_____

_____

_____

_____

_____

I LEARNED THAT…

_____

_____

_____

Tip: *No pain, no gain!*

[2] Bridges, William. Managing Transition

PONDER THIS$_{35}$
Nothing Happens Before the Time
"For when the Disciple is ready the Master is ready also."
Mabel Collins

BAR: IMPATIENCE

I first heard a variation of this quote from a friend. We were meeting for lunch and while I was sharing some of the challenges that I was facing, she said out of the blue, *"When the Student is ready, the Teacher will appear."* Initially, I was not sure what this meant but it stuck with me. I thought that the teacher was a person but I later realized that the teacher or master - depends upon the version of the quote you are reading - could also be a life experience.

So what does this saying mean? It means that we will not receive the lessons that life sends our way – via a person or situation – until the time is right and we are ready to embrace it. I will use the popular story about the hole that many of you may have heard. It goes like this.

A man was walking down a street and there was a big hole in the sidewalk.
  i.   *He did not see it so he fell into it. He eventually found his way out.*
  ii. *The man goes walking down the street another time and pretends not to see the hole. Once again, he falls into it. He gets himself out of the hole again.*
  iii. *The man goes walking down the same road with the hole in the sidewalk a third time. This time he sees it and is aware of it but falls in anyhow. It is now a habit. He finally gets out of the hole.*
  iv. *Here he goes again, down the same street with the deep hole*

in the sidewalk. This time he sees it and walks around it. He doesn't want to make the same mistake again.

v. *In the future whenever he goes for walks he goes down a different street.*

Many of us are like the man in the story. We go down the same path several times and make the same mistakes. Initially, we are not aware of it and its outcome, other times we are aware but do it anyway expecting to get a different result. Finally, we realize that what we are doing has to change in order to get the desired result we are looking for. That is when the master/teacher appears and we learn a new way. Can you relate? I sure can!

Grab your pen and paper let's go to work.

1. **Can you relate to the journey that the man travelled until he finally overcame his hole** – *situation or mistake he repeatedly made?* **Using the example above, write your journey to overcome a hole that was in your life.**

_____

_____

_____

_____

_____

_____

_____

_____

_____

_____

_____

_____

_____

_____

_____

_____

_____

_____

_____

_____

_____

_____

2. **Name your new street and your reason for choosing this name?**

_____

_____

_____

_____

_____

_____

I LEARNED THAT…

_____

_____

_____

Tip: I will use lessons learned from my past to inform my future.

PONDER THIS[36]

They Didn't Do Anything Wrong!

"Sometimes, you have to get angry to get things done."

Ang Lee

BAR: EMOTIONS

ANGER

Faith Saunders

It starts with a feeling of *ANNOYANCE*
One that continuously *NAGS* at one's being
It *GROWS* until it seems too overpowering
Consuming all of one's *ENERGY*
And *RELINQUISHING* all of one's joy.
So ...
Be *Aware* of your feelings
Nurture each one as it emerges
Genuinely and honestly *Explore* them
Because it is a sign to *Reexamine* your path.

♥

This is one emotion that we can all relate to - anger. We know what it feels like and it is not a nice feeling. How it's expressed differs from one person to the other. Of equal importance is how we use it to help us to grow. Years ago, I read – no! listened to - a book on CD by Dr. Stacey Patton – *"That Mean Old Yesterday."* It is an autobiography by a young woman who was in foster care. It is a great read or listen!

What struck me was how she used her anger, and believe me she had the right to be angry for what she went through with her step parents. So, not to give away the storyline, I won't say what she initially planned to express her anger. However, if her plans had come to fruition she would literally be in a different place and space than she is today. Someone, somewhere was watching and intervened. Long story short, she has her doctorate, writes for many news publications, is an advocate for children and does much wonderful work.

Ask yourself the following questions:
1. **What am I angry about?**

_____

_____

_____

_____

_____

_____

_____

2. **How do I express my anger? Is it healthy or self-destructive?**

_____

_____

_____

_____

_____

_____

3. **What lessons am I supposed to learn?**

_____

_____

_____

_____

_____

_____

_____

_____

4. *(If applicable)* **What was my intention?**

_____

_____

_____

_____

_____

_____

_____

_____

I LEARNED THAT…

_____

_____

_____

Tips: *I am responsible for how I feel.*

PONDER THIS₃₇

It's Okay to Make Mistakes
**"So go ahead. Fall down. The world looks different
from the ground."**
Oprah Winfrey

BAR: FEAR OF MAKING MISTAKES

Fear of failure prevents many people from fulfilling their life's dreams and aspirations. Failing is not that bad, it gives us new information. For instance, it tells us what is working and what isn't. It also gives us a new perspective and opens up new opportunities that we otherwise would not have seen.

So... what would be the worst that would happen if you failed?

_____

_____

_____

_____

_____

_____

_____

_____

_____

_____

I LEARNED THAT...

_____

_____

Tip: *"Turn your wounds into wisdom."* - Oprah Winfrey

PONDER THIS₃₈

Just Do It!

"Don't put off what you can do today for tomorrow because tomorrow may never come."

Unknown

BAR: PROCRASTINATION

I sometimes wonder how different my life would look if I did not give into the *"I don't feel like it"* trap! Recently I read that this makes a big difference between people who are very successful and others who aspire to be. The former group will **JUST DO IT! (Whatever "IT" is).** Even if they may not feel like doing **IT.** While the latter gives into their **"I don't feel like it!"** mood.

When I was growing up, my mother used to say, *"Don't put off what you can do today for tomorrow because tomorrow may never come."* If only, I had listened to her earlier. Truth be told, I fell into the latter group for a long time and sometimes revert to my old ways. I procrastinate and put off things that would help me progress. But, why do we put off the things that we are supposed to be doing? The answer varies for each of us, so I can only speak for myself. Most of the time for me it was self-doubt! Not feeling that I would be successful if I went ahead and did it!

Mother Teresa's Story

Mother Teresa, as many of you know, was a Roman Catholic nun. She is known all over the world for her life's work of caring for the poor in Calcutta, India. Not only did she care for the needy but she gave them hope. After she died, it was revealed that this woman of service and known heroine had deep-seated spiritual doubt. **What distinguishes her from many, then** and now, is that her doubts didn't prevent her from taking **ACTION.**

Next time when your inner voice says, *"I don't feel like it"*, I challenge you to JUST DO IT! (Whatever IT is). Studies show that when we act differently than how we feel, our feelings eventually catch up. I have done this and it's true. A great book for you avid readers is *Thank God You're Lazy! The Instant Cure for What's Holding You Back* by Mike Tully and Dr. Rob Gilbert. It is an easy read and has some great tips to get you moving.
Something to ponder!

1. **What is behind your, *"I don't feel like it?"***

_____

_____

_____

_____

_____

_____

_____

_____

2. **What excuses do you often use to talk yourself out of following through?**

_____

_____

_____

_____

_____

_____

_____

_____

_____

_____

3. **What are 3 positive things that could happen if you JUST DID IT and didn't give into this self-sabotaging habit?**

_____

_____

_____

_____

_____

_____

_____

_____

_____

I LEARNED THAT...

_____

_____

_____

Tip: I will override my, *"I don't feel like it"* by just DOING IT (whatever IT is)!

PONDER THIS$_{39}$
What Type of Lover Are You?
"When we feel love and kindness toward others, it not only makes others feel loved and cared for, but it helps us also to develop inner happiness and peace."

Dalai Lama XIV

BAR: RELATIONSHIPS

I got your attention! Yes, this is about love, but in the context of how you are showing up in the world. I was listening to Tony Robbins, and he spoke about various types of love and how, as adults, we use these various types of love to get what we want in life. Some people use a combination of them based upon the situation, and others spend their time stuck on one.

Types of Love
1. *Baby Love* – This is quite the opposite of what I originally thought it was. We all know that babies are cute and charming (here is the punch line) when they are getting what they want. As soon as their needs are not being met, they stop being cute! They cry and whine nonstop until their needs are satisfied. **We love as long as our needs are being met.**

2. *Conditional Love* – Initially this sounds like Baby Love but the difference is that we have a covert operation going. In other words, we act as if what we are doing is genuine, out of love but unbeknown to others we are expecting something in return. When we do not get what we want, we then get upset (and some of us even act up). **We love with strings attached.**

3. *Real Love* – Have you met someone and thanked them for something that they did and they looked at you like you had 10 heads. They had no clue what you were referring to. This is genuine love, with no expectations. **You give of yourself because of who you are. There are no strings attached to**

Page | **121**

what you do.

4. *Spiritual Love* – This is what the Bible refers to as Agape love. It is loving others despite the pain and hurt that they have caused you and/or others. This is the highest level of love and not many people practice this on a daily basis. Tony used Nelson Mandela as an example of someone who has demonstrated this type of love. **You love despite the wrong and/or hurt that was done to you.**

We are all human and we have practiced all or most of these types of love at some point in our lives.

What type of love do you practice most often - Baby Love, Conditional Love, Real Love or Spiritual Love? Give an example. Now, tell the truth!

_____

_____

_____

_____

_____

_____

_____

_____

_____

_____

_____

_____

_____

_____

_____

What are some of the challenges that get in the way of you practicing *Real Love or Spiritual Love* most of the time?

_____

_____

_____

_____

_____

_____

_____

_____

_____

_____

_____

_____

_____

Tip: I will consciously work to upgrade my love to be more SPIRITUAL.

What Is Your Vision?
"You can have it all. Just not all at once."
Oprah Winfrey

BAR: LACK OF VISION

Most successful companies have a vision statement; however, it is something that as individuals, many people don't even think about, yet have. So what exactly is a vision statement? It is a sentence or short concise paragraphs that help you to identify your goals. It answers the question, **"Where am I going?"** or **"What will I do or want to do?"** It guides your life and provides direction regarding what course you will take. In other words, if done right, it becomes a filter that all decisions are funneled through.

Sometimes people mistakenly believe that a mission and vision statement are one and the same. However, they are not. The mission statement answers the questions - *"Why am I here?"* and *"Why do I exist?"* As mention above, the vision statement takes things a step further. It helps the person to live their purpose.

Below are my personal mission and vision statements along with my thought process behind them.

- My Personal Mission Statement: *To live from the inside out at all times.*
  Rationale: I believe that God lives with in me and for me to be the best person I can be it is imperative that I connect with the essence of who I am.

- My Personal Vision Statement: *To live life on my terms by being the best version of myself and doing what makes me happy so I can make a difference in the world.*

  Rationale: If I am living life from the inside out (my mission), I am continuously connecting with my Higher

Power. Hence, I work hard not to make fear and other "prison bars" hold me hostage. Do I falter? Definitely! I am human. Working through the fear allows me to live life on my term and show up authentically (my vision).

We are all a work in progress so this journey is not a linear one.

There are many benefits of having a personal vision statement.

1. CLARITY – A vision statement helps us to decipher what we need to do to fulfill our true purpose. Otherwise, we can waste precious time doing mundane things that takes us off our path.

2. FOCUS – A vision statement helps us to pay attention to what's really important in our life.

3. AUTHENTICITY - A vision statement assists us in becoming self-aware and connect with our authentic self.

4. BUILD CONFIDENCE - A clear vision statement helps us to reframe our opinion about ourselves so it is more positive. In addition, the successes that we have along the way build on each other and build our confidence.

WORDS OF CAUTION:

If done properly, this will take you quite a while to do. Don't rush it. Trust the process and take the time needed to craft a statement that will drive you to where you want to go.

Aristotle once said, *"The soul never thinks without a picture."* Now, take the time to paint a picture that your soul can follow.

Identify 5 things that you most enjoy doing on a daily, weekly, monthly, and yearly basis without which you would feel incomplete.

a. _____

_____

b. _____

_____

c. _____

_____

d. _____

_____

e. _____

In the next 10 years, I want ...

- to be and do: _____

_____

_____

- to know: _____

_____

_____

- to be associated with: _____

_____

_____

- to have the following impact on my family: _____

_____

_____

- to have the following impact on my community and/or society: _____

_____

_____

My Personal Vision Statement:

_____

_____

_____

_____

_____

_____

_____

_____

_____

_____

_____

_____

_____

_____

_____

I LEARNED THAT…

_____

_____

_____

Tip: *Own your vision – turn it into reality!*

PONDER THIS₄₁
What Do You See?
"Your perception is your reality."
Unknown

BAR: HEADTRASH

Is this glass half full or half empty? Explain

_____

_____

_____

_____

How we perceive things is directly related to how we respond to them. Let me explain. If I perceive this glass to be half full and that there is more water where this came from, I am looking at it from a viewpoint of abundance. I may drink it all at once or even throw it away. If, on the other hand, I perceive it to be empty and there is not more where this came from, I am looking at it from a shortage perspective and will definitely respond differently. For instance, I may only take small sips to ensure that it last for a long time.

The important thing is to remember to make sure that your perception is not distorted because you are looking at them through dirty lens. What do I mean? Sometimes the bars (that you identified in the first exercise) may distort your vision. As a result, you make decisions that are not in your best interest and could hurt you and those you love and care about.

Now go back and look at the prison bars you identified in the first exercise. Using your top 3, take a few minutes and think how each could have influenced your early response to the question, *"Is this glass half full or half empty!"*

Prison Bar #1:

_____

_____

Impact on answer:

_____

_____

_____

_____

_____

_____

_____

_____

_____

_____

_____

_____

Prison Bar #2:

_____

_____

Impact on answer:

_____

_____

_____

_____

_____

_____

_____

_____

_____

_____

_____

_____

Prison Bar #3:

_____

_____

Impact on answer:

_____

_____

_____

_____

_____

_____

_____

_____

I LEARNED THAT…

_____

_____

Tip: How we perceive our world is directly related to the lens that we are seeing it through.

YOU HAVE TO

BE

BEFORE YOU CAN DO,

DO

BEFORE YOU

HAVE

Zig Ziglar

PONDER THIS₄₂

You're Responsible for Your Wellness
**"Wellness is the complete integration of body, mind, and spirit
- the realization that everything we do, think, feel, and believe
has an effect on our state of well-being."**
Greg Anderson

BAR: LACK OF FORESIGHT

There is a model called the Dimension of Wellness. This model states that there are 8 key areas of our life that we need to pay attention to if we want to live a balanced life. The following diagram identifies each Dimension of Wellness and what each means.

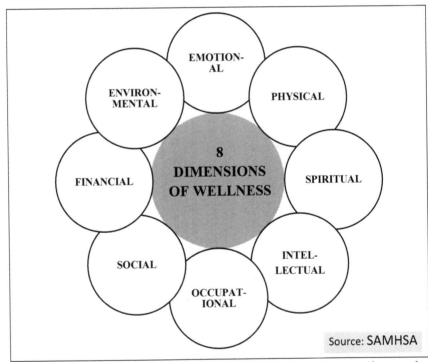

Explanation of each Dimension of Wellness as per the *Substance Abuse and Mental Health Services Administration (SAMHSA)*

1. **EMOTIONAL:** *Coping effectively with life and creating satisfying relationships.*
2. **PHYSICAL:** *Recognizing the need for physical activities, diet, sleep and nutrition.*
3. **SPIRITUAL:** *Expanding our sense of purpose and meaning in life.*
4. **INTELLECTUAL:** *Recognizing creative abilities and finding ways to expand knowledge and skills.*
5. **OCCUPATIONAL:** *Personal satisfaction and enrichment derived from one's work.*
6. **SOCIAL:** *Developing a sense of connection, belonging, and a well-developed support system.*
7. **FINANCIAL:** *Satisfaction with current and future financial situations.*
8. **ENVIRONMENTAL:** *Good health by occupying pleasant, stimulating environments that support well-being.*

Each of these dimensions are interrelated. A change in one will impact the other. So for example, a person who has no money to pay her bills *(financial dimension)*, may become stressed out and even depressed *(emotional dimension)*, which leads to her withdrawing and isolating *(social dimension)*, she starts calling out from work and her productivity starts to go down *(occupational dimension)*, she starts to doubting her purpose *(spiritual dimension)* and so forth. Get it?

My son, asked me a question that I am going to ask you - *"What will you do today that your future self will thank you for?"* Powerful question right? Using this question as the premise for the following exercise, write what you are going to do each day to improve your wellness in the following areas.

DAY #1: _____ *(insert date)*

What will you do today to improve your EMOTIONAL WELLNESS that your future self will thank you for?

_____

_____

_____

_____

Will your future self thank you? (In other words, did you do what you said you would do?)
COMMENT:

_____

_____

_____

_____

DAY #2: _____ *(insert date)*

What will you do today to improve your OCCUPATIONAL WELLNESS that your future self will thank you for?

_____

_____

_____

_____

Will your future self thank you? (In other words, did you do what you said you would do?)
COMMENT:

_____

_____

_____

_____

DAY #3: _____ *(insert date)*

What will you do today to improve your PHYSICAL WELLNESS that your future self will thank you for?

_____

_____

_____

_____

Will your future self thank you? (In other words, did you do what you said you would do?)
COMMENT:

_____

_____

_____

_____

DAY #4: _____ *(insert date)*

What will you do today to improve your SPIRITUAL WELL-NESS that your future self will thank you for?

_____

_____

_____

_____

Will your future self thank you? (In other words, did you do what you said you would do?)
COMMENT:

_____

_____

_____

_____

DAY #5: _____ _(insert date)_

What will you do today to improve your FINANCIAL WELLNESS that your future self will thank you for?

_____

_____

_____

_____

Will your future self thank you? (In other words, did you do what you said you would do?)
COMMENT:

_____

_____

_____

_____

DAY #6: _____ _(insert date)_

What will you do today to improve your ENVIRONMENTAL WELLNESS that your future self will thank you for?

_____

_____

_____

_____

Will your future self thank you? (In other words, did you do what you said you would do?)
COMMENT:

_____

_____

_____

_____

DAY #7: _____ *(insert date)*

What will you do today to improve your **INTELLECTUAL WELLNESS** that your future self will thank you for?

_____

_____

_____

_____

Will your future self thank you? (In other words, did you do what you said you would do?)
COMMENT:

_____

_____

_____

_____

DAY #8: _____ *(insert date)*

What will you do today to improve your **SOCIAL WELLNESS** that your future self will thank you for?

_____

_____

_____

_____

Will your future self thank you? (In other words, did you do what you said you would do?)
COMMENT:

_____

_____

I LEARNED THAT…

Tip: *"FACT - If standard of living is your number one objective, quality of life almost never improves. But if quality of life is your number one objective, standard of living invariably improves."*
Zig Ziglar

PONDER THIS₄₃

Making a Statement

"My life will not be an apology. It will be a statement!"

Andy Andrews

BAR: REGRETS

As of this moment, how do you see your life - a series of **apologies** or does it make **a statement**? *Explain your answer.*

_____

_____

_____

_____

_____

_____

_____

_____

_____

_____

_____

_____

_____

_____

_____

_____

_____

_____

_____

_____

_____

_____

_____

_____

_____

_____

_____

_____

_____

_____

_____

_____

_____

I LEARNED THAT…

_____

_____

_____

Tip: *I was created to make a BOLD statement!*

PONDER THIS[44]

Without HOPE We Have Nothing!
"The inability to open up to HOPE is what blocks trust, and blocked trust is the reason for blighted dreams."
Elizabeth Gilbert

BAR: DEPRESSION

According to the Webster dictionary HOPE is *"to want something to happen or be true **and** think that it could happen or be true."* In other words, hope is not only wanting, but what really gets us moving is our *belief* that it can/will happen.

This leads me to my next question, *"Is it lack of BELIEF, as defined by Mr. Webster, the reason why so many of us shy away from pursuing our goals and deepest aspirations?"* In my mind's eyes, hope is that one thing that pulls us through the tough times. It is the foundation of all inventions. Everything begins with a thought in someone's mind. For instance - the phone! Today, we cannot leave home without it! But if Alexander Graham Bell did not **want his invention to become a reality AND believed that it would allow people to communicate when they were not face to face**, I wonder what the world would be like today?

What do you HOPE for – remember this involves not only wanting but believing that it can happen?

_____

_____

_____

_____

_____

_____

_____

_____

_____

_____

_____

_____

_____

_____

_____

_____

_____

_____

_____

_____

_____

I LEARNED THAT…

_____

_____

_____

Tip: *I am not only hopeful but I also believe my dreams*
will become a reality!

PONDER THIS[45]

Who is in Your Corner?

"Make your relationships an '8' or better?"

John Salunek

BAR: LACK OF SUPPORT

I heard someone say once that many of us take more time when we are purchasing a pair of shoes to make sure that it is the right size, color, etc., than we do when choosing our friends. Some friendships change as we grow physically, emotion and spiritually.

Like a pair of shoes that used to fit, they don't fit anymore. For instance, they're no longer comfortable, we have worn them too often and no matter how we fix them, they fall apart – I think you get what I am saying. In human terms – as our values, interests and likes change so does our compatibility. The problem for many of us is that we hold on to relationships - platonic and intimate ones - that are not working because *(you fill in the rest)* ______________________________

____

____

It's time to reevaluate your relationships.

****Rate your primary relationship on a scale of 1 *(unhealthy)* - 10 *(healthy)*?**

Friend's Name	Rate** [1-10]	Reason	Next Step

I LEARNED THAT…

_____

_____

_____

Tip: *I will be more mindful of the company I keep.*

PONDER THIS₄₆

PONDER THIS₄₆

Be Grateful

"As we express our gratitude, we must never forget that the highest appreciation is not to utter words, but to live by them."

John F. Kennedy

BAR: UNGRATEFULNESS

It's strange that some of the most powerful statements are made up of few words. Before we go any further, I think it is imperative to focus our attention on gratitude. So often we focus on the things that are NOT going well in our lives and overlook the things that ARE GOING WELL. I believe that being grateful is another vehicle that helps to pull us through difficult times. It helps us to see things from a different perspective – not doom and gloom but from a positive standpoint.

Let me use an example to explain. Let's take you for instance; yes you - my new friend! There are things that are not going well in your life at this moment. No, wait! Don't close the book! You may be thinking, *"Faith is presumptuous to think that there is something in my life that is not going well!"* I am not. Like all of us, you are alive and this privilege comes with challenges.

I am here to say that despite what you are facing in your life, there are many things that you can be grateful for. Let's count some of them:

1. You can see
2. You are able to read
3. You are able to think
4. You're of sound mind

I could go on and on.

Approaching our challenges from a gratitude perspective gives it a different picture. I was coaching someone who was looking for employment. She came to one of our sessions really down because she had not been hearing back from employers. She started beating upon herself by saying things like, *"I will never get a job."* So I gave her the following exercise to write 10 things that you are grateful for. This is what she wrote:

I am grateful that ...
1. *I am alive*
2. *I am in good health*
3. *I have a roof over my head*
4. *I have food to eat and not hungry*
5. *I have a coach that can help me with my job search*
6. *I have a car that is working*
7. *I have skills and experience that I can use to get a job*
8. *I have supportive family and friends*
9. *There are jobs that I can apply for*
10. *I am being called in to come in on interviews.*

She went on to say that this exercise put things into perspective for her because it is so easy to focus on the challenges at hand, and forget the other things that are going well.

Personally, I find that when I express gratitude I feel better. In a sense it calms me because, in the bigger scheme of things, my problems seems much smaller and less overwhelming! Nine times out of ten, tentative solutions to my problem emerges.

It's your turn!
List 10 things that you are grateful for. *Challenge - don't mention anything that was mentioned before.*

1. _____

   _____

2. _____

3. _____

4. _____

5. _____

6. _____

7. _____

8. _____

9. _____

10. _____

CHALLENGE: Before you go to sleep each night, identify at least 1 thing that occurred during the day for which you are grateful. You'll be surprised how this will impact your life.

I LEARNED THAT…

_____

_____

Tip: *"True happiness comes from a grateful heart."*
Andy Andrews

PONDER THIS$_{47}$

It Starts with a Plan
"Four steps to ACHIEVEMENT
PLAN Purposefully! PREPARE prayerfully! PROCEED positively! PURSUE persistently!"
William Arthur Ward

BAR: POOR PLANNING

In order to achieve our goals we have to have a PLAN. However, this plan must have clear and achievable outcomes which involves the **three C's - COMMITMENT, CONSISTENCY and CALCULATION.** What do I mean?

COMMITMENT – Make a decision that you are going to do what it takes to make this change. As mentioned several times in earlier chapters, for us to make this commitment we must believe that it POSITIVE and POSSIBLE. In other words, whatever change we are going to make, we must see the ultimate outcome to be significantly positive and believe that we are capable of accomplishing it.

CONSISTENCY – When I was growing up with my siblings in Jamaica, my mom often said when we exhibited a behavior that was not appropriate that "practice makes perfect." What she meant was that if we continue the behavior at home, we would do the action outside of our home, even though we know it was wrong, because we were so used to doing it. The same applies here. This change is going to require practice. Practicing the new ways of thinking and doing will result in them eventually becoming habits.

CALCULATION – There must be some way to measure your progress. In PONDER THIS$_{34}$, we used an example of losing 30 pounds as our goal. How would you know if you achieved your goal if you don't weigh yourself on a scale? Furthermore, visually seeing the gradual weight loss will motivate you to keep going.

So, are you ready to make lasting change?

COMMITMENT: Identify one change you are committed to make in the next 3 months.

_____

_____

_____

_____

_____

_____

_____

_____

_____

CONSISTENCY: Identify the ACTION STEPS you will need to take for this change to become a new habit. _(Also include when you will do it and how frequently you will do each action.)_

_____

_____

_____

_____

_____

_____

_____

_____

_____

_____

_____

Identify who will be your SUPPORT/ACCOUNTABILITY PARTNER during this change.

_____

_____

_____

_____

_____

CALCULATION: How will you measure your progress?

_____

_____

_____

_____

_____

I LEARNED THAT…

_____

_____

_____

Tip: I will plan ahead.

Money Matters

"It's not what you earn but what you save that matters."

Violet Lennox

BAR: POOR SPENDING HABITS

When I first came to the United States, I was financially broke. For the first 5 years, I worked as a live in housekeeper. My first job was working with a family on Park Avenue in New York City. The lady who I used to work with was a family friend from Jamaica and I will never forget what she told me when I started to work. It is a principle that I live my life by. She said, *"Faith, remember, it is not what you earn but what you save."* What she meant was that no matter what I earned, it was imperative that I saved something, no matter how small.

Many of us grew up hearing many negative things about money. Most of which tarnish how we perceive and relate to money. Two that were frequently used when I was a child were:

- Money is the root of all evil.
- Rich people are dishonest.

For a long time, these two sayings played havoc on my mind. I did save but was terrified that if I had wealth it would ruin my character. Talk about headtrash! After much work, I am coming to embrace the value money can give. It can liberate one to make a significant positive impact on this world.

So what's your relationship with money?

1. **What messages did you hear about money when you were growing up?**

_____

_____

_____

_____

2. How have these messages impacted your relationship with money?

_____

_____

_____

_____

3. To get a glimpse of your relationship as it relates to your spending habits, for the next 7 days, write down everything you spend using cash, debit and/or credit card. *(Use extra paper if needed)*
   <u>EXAMPLE</u>

   7/28/15 - Met June for dinner at Panera Bread - Credit Card - $50

_____

_____

_____

_____

_____

_____

_____

_____

_____

_____

_____

_____

_____

_____

_____

_____

_____

_____

_____

_____

_____

_____

_____

_____

_____

_____

_____

_____

_____

_____

4. Categorize your purchases – *Food, Entertainment, Gas, Clothes, etc.* – this will help you to see where you are spending your money. Total

<u>EXAMPLE</u>

Category	Total Amount Spent
Food	*$400*

_____ _____
_____ _____
_____ _____
_____ _____
_____ _____
_____ _____
_____ _____
_____ _____
_____ _____
_____ _____

TOTAL $_____

5. **Now that you have a glimpse of your spending habits – are you surprised about anything?** *Explain*

_____

_____

_____

_____

6. **What, if any changes, will you make?**

_____

_____

_____

_____

I LEARNED THAT…

_____

_____

_____

Tip: *If you respect your money it will respect you.*

PONDER THIS₄₉

You Only Have Control Over YOURSELF
"You cannot control what happens to you, but you can control your attitude toward what happens to you, and in that, you will be mastering change rather than allowing it to master you."

Brian Tracy

BAR: MISGUIDED FOCUS

Have you ever asked the Universe to help you with a problem but take it back by stressing and obsessing about it? I don't know about you but I am guilty as charged!

In the past, I often wondered why I did this. Tony Robbins say that one of the reasons why we try to control our circumstances is that we are wired for order. When we feel out of control, we have a natural tendency to create structure. The big problem is there are so many moving parts – most of which we are not aware of and don't have control over - that we are basically trying to accomplish the impossible. Some things that are out of our control includes what other people, think, say or do. However, don't be dismayed, there is one thing that we have control over that we neglect – OUR minds and behaviors. If we remember this, and practice mastering these two things, we would avoid a great deal of unnecessary stress.

I love the *Serenity Prayer* because it helps us to see how power**LESS** we are on one hand and how power**FUL** we are on the other.

Below is a poem that I wrote many years ago (according to my notes - April 5, 1999 to be exact). It uses the *Serenity Prayer* as its foundation.

Grant me the SERENITY to accept the things I cannot change
But to offer support in realistic ways

Always remembering that we are all given
Our share of trials to bear
So that we can grow stronger each day

The COURAGE to change the things that I can
Cause I only have control over me
I can put myself in situations and around people who are positive
I can change the way that I think and feel
And step forward in faith

And the WISDOM to know the difference
I can look at the positive instead of the negative
Focus on strengths rather than weaknesses
Look ahead but do not forget the past
Because there is a lot to learn from it
Love myself and share with others
Support but do not carry!

What/who are some of the situations/people that you have been trying to control? Give an example of how you have tried to control this situation/person? How successful have you been doing this - explain.

Situation/person: _____

_____

Example of ways you have tried to be in control

_____

_____

_____

_____

_____

_____

Outcome: _____

_____

_____

_____

_____

How could you have responded differently? _____

_____

_____

_____

I LEARNED THAT...

_____

_____

Tip: *I will focus on what I have control over - my thoughts and actions.*

Success Is A Subjective Word
**"The key to success isn't what you do.
It's how you feel about what you're doing."**
Iyanla Vanzant

BAR: COMPARING ONESELF TO OTHERS

We are part of a very materialistic and self-centered culture which is not bad. The problem arises when we start comparing ourselves to others - what they have and what they are doing. When I was growing up in Jamaica, my mother often cautioned us, her children, not to chase after things because other people have them. Her rationale was that we did not know how they came by it. Another important question to ask oneself is why do we *wanted* it. I emphasize the word WANT because most of the time the stuff we acquire we don't need.

Many people use these terms – want and need - interchangeably but they are different. A **need** is something that is extremely necessary for a person to survive. If a need is not met, a person could become ill, unable to function or even die. Examples of a need are food, water, shelter, air, etc.

On the other hand, a want is something that a person desires, either immediately or in the future. Wants differ from one person to another. For example, one person may want to own a car, while another may want to travel to an exotic country. Unlike needs which are constant, our wants change and their level of importance also varies.

In order to know whether what you desire is a want or a need, ask this basic and fundamental question: **"Have you been able to survive without this?"** If your answer is 'yes', then what you desire is a want, no matter how much you crave for it right now.

You may be wondering, '*Why is it important to discern between a want and a need?*' The answer is motive. If you are yearning after something that is not a need – why is it important to you? This ties back to Zig Ziglar's quote - **"You have to 'BE' before you can 'DO,' and do before you can HAVE."**

In other words - is this want to satisfy your need to BE? If so, you'll be constantly chasing after things to feel fulfilled which can be very expensive and don't work. My hope is that after doing all the work in this book – this is not the case.

Now that you have done the work, what does success mean to you?

_____

_____

_____

_____

_____

_____

_____

_____

_____

_____

_____

I LEARNED THAT…

_____

_____

_____

Tip: *Question the motives behind your thoughts and actions.*

PONDER THIS₅₁

Time to Play

"All work and no play makes Jack a dull boy."

James Howell

BAR: IMBALANCE

There is one thing that children do naturally - even us, if we allow our self to reminisce. That is PLAY. For some reason, many of us (and I have to include myself) take life too seriously and forget to play. As you read further, you'll see that this often ignored part of life has serious consequences.

One person who has spent decades studying the topic is Dr. Stewart Brown. In his book, *Play*, Dr. Brown describes play to the oxygen that we breathe. He has studied various groups, such as, inmates, businesspeople and Nobel Prize winners and uncovered a number of interesting findings. For instance, play can

- Rekindle the relationship of couples and lead to the exploration of other emotional intimacy.
- Facilitate the creation of deep relationship between strangers.
- Foster healing of emotional wounds

There are other benefits of playing and they include:

- Relieve stress
- Improve brain function
- Stimulate the mind and boost creativity
- Keep you feeling young and energetic
- Helps develop and improve social skills
- Teaches cooperation with others

What is Play?

Dr. Brown says that play is *a state of being*. It is not a thing but a process. In other words, it is an experience not a goal. Play should be "purposeless, fun and pleasurable."

How to Play

This may sound weird but it is an area many adults struggle with –
especially *moi* (French word for me). Dr. Brown states that we
should put aside time to play every day and a little play can go a
long way. Based upon the above description - it is not a thing. It is
a process that is purposeless, fun and pleasurable. Therefore, what
is fun for one person will not be fun to another. For instance, some
people find knitting to be fun because it relaxes them; however, it
is torture to someone else.

Tips to enhance your play repertoire:

1. Pay attention to the things that relax you and bring you
   joy. For instance - walking your dog, *daydreaming*.
   Yes, daydreaming is a form of play as long as you
   enjoy it.
2. Surround yourself with playful people. It's hard not to
   get involved when other people around you are doing
   things you consider fun. However, be open to new
   opportunities - you never know if you will find a new
   fun activity.
3. Play with kids. Allow yourself to be kidlike when
   playing with children. We all have an inner kid who
   wants to play if we give him/her permission to.

How do you play?

_____

_____

_____

_____

_____

_____

_____

_____

Expand your play repertoire by answering the following questions.
What did you do as a child that exited you?
Did you engage in these activities alone, with others or both?

_____

_____

_____

_____

_____

_____

_____

_____

_____

_____

_____

_____

_____

How can you recreate these today?

_____

_____

_____

_____

_____

_____

_____

_____

_____

_____

_____

_____

_____

I LEARNED THAT…

_____

_____

_____

Tip: *Take time to play!*

PONDER THIS₅₂

You Matter

"My mission in life is not merely to survive, but to thrive; and to do so with some passion, some compassion, some humor, and some style."

Maya Angelou

BAR: WHAT FOLLOWS "I Am…"

CAUTION: Do <u>NOT</u> read what you previously wrote until <u>AFTER</u> you have done this exercise.

In **PONDER THIS₂** you wrote about how you saw yourself. Now that you have done the work and have come to know yourself better, please do the activity again.

Find a quiet space and in your journal/notebook complete the following sentence. Don't think, just write for 15 minutes anything that comes to mind. You'll be surprised what shows up on paper! *Use additional paper if you needed.*

"I AM …

_____

_____

_____

_____

_____

_____

_____

_____

_____

_____

_____

_____

_____

_____

_____

_____

_____

_____

_____

_____

_____

_____

_____

I LEARNED THAT…

_____

_____

_____

Tip: *Embrace your greatness!*

CONGRATULATIONS!

You did it! I know that it was not easy completing this book but I really hope it was worth it! I recommend that you repeat the activities occasionally. We are ever evolving and your response will inevitable change as time goes by and you can gain new insight. In addition, we are humans, creatures of habit; hence, with the best intensions, we sometimes revert to old behaviors. Reviewing your responses could put you back on track.

I would love to hear from you. Please feel free to contact me. I can be reached at:
- **discoveranewfuture@gmail.com**
- **http://www.facebook.com/discoveranewfuture**
- **www.linkedin.com/in/faithsaunders/**
- **www.discoveranewfuture.com**

Much blessings!

UNTIL NEXT TIME…
Think Positively!

Made in the USA
Middletown, DE
07 April 2016